Navigating the Talent Shift

Lisa Hufford

Navigating the Talent Shift

How to Build On-Demand Teams that Drive Innovation, Control Costs, and Get Results

2Lisa Hufford
Simplicity Consulting
Kirkland, Washington, USA

ISBN 978-1-137-54803-0   ISBN 978-1-137-54802-3   (eBook)
DOI 10.1057/978-1-137-54802-3

Library of Congress Control Number: 2016945576

Printed on acid-free paper

This Palgrave Macmillan imprint is published by Springer Nature
The registered company is Nature America Inc. New York

For my supportive and loving husband, David, and our beautiful boys, Jack and Ian. You inspire me to live an authentic and purpose-driven life.

Contents

Acknowledgments

This book is a true collective effort of so many talented people who I have been fortunate to know and work with.

I have been able to develop my expertise because of the thousands of consultants and clients whom I have had the honor of listening to, coaching, advising, and learning from in the course of growing my business. I am grateful to all of you who contributed your time and experiences to this book so that other professionals can learn from your wisdom.

Thank you to the entire Simplicity Consulting staff, who have shared their vision with me and shown their commitment to providing an exceptional customer experience in every conversation and interaction. Specifically, thank you, Carrie Morris. You have been my chief cheerleader, motivator, and strategic doer at Simplicity Consulting. Nobody thinks bigger than you, and you believed in the idea of this book even before I did. Your contagious enthusiasm infects everyone you interact with, and I am grateful for your shared vision, brainstorming sessions, and passion to continue to do more and better.

Special thanks to the many previous managers who have shaped, enabled, and supported my growth and development over the 20+ years of my working life. I am fortunate to have learned valuable leadership lessons from each of them and am grateful for the opportunities that they have provided me.

My advisors, Dr. Pamela Peeke and Rick Wong, for their unwavering confidence in me, for having my back, offering advice and their broad perspective.

My brand strategist and writer, Elizabeth Kanna, and writer, William DiBenedetto, who bring the soul and narrative of my ideas to life. Our goal was to create a practical, approachable business book like no other, and your creative talents have made it a reality.

Laurie Harting, executive editor at Palgrave Macmillan, for her keen ideas and insight that have contributed to this book being a game changer.

My business owner peers and close friends, on whom I rely on for sanity checks and advice, and my Young Presidents' Organization (YPO) forum for their unconditional support and contribution to my growth as a business leader.

Academic leaders, including Sandeep Krishnamurthy of Dean Business School UW Bothell, and Scott Dawson of Dean Business School Cal Poly San Luis Obispo, for their unrelenting support of entrepreneurial ideas and focus on making the world a better place.

Thought leaders who I have never met but admire from afar and who have shaped my thoughts and actions, including Seth Godin, Dan Pink, Stephen Covey, Oprah Winfrey, Greg McKeown, and Simon Sinek.

My parents for their unconditional love and support of whatever I chose to do throughout my life; they told me I could do anything and I believed them.

My extended family and dear friends who fill my soul with laughter and happiness.

Introduction

I wrote *Navigating the Talent Shift* to help companies redefine how to meet their business and workplace objectives, drive innovation, and build flexible teams in a project-based environment that tap into a broader talent pool.

Companies can be more competitive and adapt faster to changing market needs by integrating into their teams the broad and growing base of freelancers and consultants. My vision is that companies will expand their mindset about how they access and acquire the talent they need to achieve the best results in any business climate. And I believe that professionals can find significance by and success by focusing on the work they love to do and adding value to every job.

We're living in an on-demand world and an on-demand economy, ranging from the movies we watch and the groceries we buy to the way we travel. Welcome to the on-demand workplace.

My Passion for Business

My parents are retired teachers. In fact, my entire family is in education and proud of it. I've always had an interest in business, even from an early age, but my parents were still surprised when I decided to major in business at California Polytechnic State University, where I received my Bachelor's degree.

After earning my degree, I worked for 14 years in the technology sector as well as earning my Technology MBA certificate from the University of Washington. I was in supply-chain management, and then worked for Microsoft—in sales, account management and business development, and running global sales teams while traveling the world. I worked for the dominant players in their industries and was fortunate to work with leading brands such as Apple, IBM, Sony, Toshiba, Sun Microsystems, and Acer, to name a few. I enjoyed finding solutions, scoring win-wins, and executing high-impact projects with large clients.

When I had my second child in 2006 something shifted for me. I wanted to figure out how to leverage my skills so that I could work on my own terms, and I wanted to control my own schedule, spend more time with my family, and cut back on my business travel.

I was in search of both a work and lifestyle change, for sure, but I also wanted more. As anyone who's spent time in corporate America knows, the average day at the office involves many activities that don't have much to do with your core competency or job description: attending superfluous meetings, playing email ping-pong, or being waylaid by chatty coworkers.

When I was a Director at Microsoft, for example, I had a myriad of responsibilities, and while I didn't mind them, they weren't what you'd consider "mission-critical." I realized I also wanted to zero in on doing more high-impact work, using a larger portion of my time on projects that made the biggest difference for companies. To achieve those things, I approached my V.P. at Microsoft and presented him with a plan and a description of how I could, as a consultant, support highly strategic initiatives for the leadership team in the division. He agreed to let me transition into a consultant role, and Microsoft was my first client. Looking back, that was a monumental moment for me.

As a consultant, I found I was able to work on projects in ways that actually delivered more impact than I'd been able to deliver in the role of a corporate director. This is because I was able to give 100% of my focus to mission-critical tasks; I didn't have all of the other, less important responsibilities that go along with being a company director to distract me.

Not long after my transition to consulting, I was approached by others with similar stories—corporate professionals who wanted more control, flexibility, and the chance to use their skills for work that really mattered. I began teaching people how to make the transition from a traditional FTE job to a consultant, and before I knew it, I had a business. My business grew quickly. I identified an emerging trend in the workforce: companies were looking to reduce cost and risk, often by slashing talent and resources vital to the business's success, but they still needed experts to get the work done. I saw an opportunity to provide companies with a cost-effective, low-risk way to tap exceptional talent. I also provided corporate professionals with the opportunity to do what I did—be in control and have a choice in their lives. It was a win-win, and I became committed to helping people find success on their terms with their clients and consultants.

Within its first 18 months, my company, Simplicity Consulting Inc., had 20 consultants. Since 2006, we have successfully completed thousands of projects with a growing community of more than 5,000 professionals. Simplicity was named to the Inc. 5000 list for five years running as one of the fastest-growing private companies in America. This growth is evidence of the workplace and talent shift that's underway.

In my work at Simplicity, I've helped companies such as Amazon, Hewlett Packard, Farmers Insurance, T-Mobile, and Microsoft create flexible teams with the on-demand experts they need to achieve their business objectives. I've worked with companies as they embraced agility and leveraged the on-demand workforce, enabling these big players to overcome multi-million-dollar challenges, transform company-wide legacy systems to stay relevant, and reinvigorate declining sales channels into $100 million dollar businesses.

What This Book Covers

The first two chapters define and describe the talent shift:

Chapter 1 describes the workforce shift that's driven by a changing global business environment, a highly competitive marketplace that features hyper-specialization, project-based work, and a talent pool that aspires to—and indeed demands—flexibility. A variety of economic, technological, and cultural factors drives this dynamic shift. The chapter examines three major trends that have converged to shape where we are: the coming of age of Millennials,[1] the Baby Boomers' impact on the workforce, and the trend that will impact about 40% of U.S. workers by 2020, the freelance "1099 economy."[2]

Chapter 2 delves deeper into the changing face of talent and notes that by 2020, as many as 65 million Americans will be freelancers, independent consultants and solopreneurs, making up 40% of the workforce. The ramifications of those numbers are enormous.

Chapters 3 and 4 introduce and describe the centerpiece of this book: the SPEED™ talent strategy that enables managers to build flexible, project-based teams that get results. SPEED provides an agile and flexible framework for building on-demand teams, and it also provides the ability to adapt to unanticipated business changes. It encompasses the best practices that I have learned, observed, and implemented in hundreds of projects with every type of cost, management, and operational situation.

Chapter 5 outlines some common roadblocks companies may encounter when integrating SPEED within their organizations and how to overcome them. I see roadblocks every day—whether it is mindset, organizational, structural, procedural, or political—and they can all be resolved.

Chapters 6, 7, and **8** feature real-world stories that show how companies have creatively used on-demand talent to drive innovation, control costs, and get results.

The Resource Guide provides you with additional resources, research, and information about the talent shift and places where you can find that talent. It also lists elements you can use to evaluate a talent agency.

Terms and Definitions

As I note in Chap. 1, there is a great workforce shift underway, driven by a constantly changing global business environment, a highly competitive marketplace that features hyper-specialization, project-based work, and a talent pool that aspires to—and indeed demands—flexibility.

I define the **talent shift** as the emerging and broad talent pool that's driving a massive change to an on-demand workforce that comprises specialists, independent professionals, and experts—however they are called—doing project-based work.

In this book, I use the term **consultant** most often, but I also use the terms "experts" and "specialists" interchangeably throughout. **Talent** as referred to in this book includes those consultants, freelancers, experts, and specialists who are all in non-FTE (full-time employee) roles.

However, the name or term for talent that are not an FTE varies depending on the publication, the industry, company policies, and even how a person refers to their own professional classification. For example, in their 2015 study, "Freelancing in America," Upwork and the Freelancers Union identified five types of freelancers, which that year composed more than one-third of the U.S. workforce.

The Five Types of Freelancers[3]

1. Independent Contractors

    (36% of the independent workforce/19.3 million professionals)—These "traditional" freelancers don't have an employer and instead do freelance, temporary, or supplemental work on a project-to-project basis.

2. Moonlighters

    (25%/13.2 million)—Moonlighters are individuals with a primary, traditional job with an employer who also moonlight doing freelance work. For example, a corporate-employed web developer who does projects for nonprofits in the evening is a moonlighter.

3. Diversified workers

    (26%/14.1 million)—Diversified workers are people with multiple sources of income from a mix of traditional employers and freelance work. For example, someone who works the front desk at a dentist's office 20 hours a week and fills out the rest of his income driving for Uber and doing freelance writing is a diversified worker.

4. Temporary Workers

    (9%/4.6 million)—Temporary workers are individuals with a single employer, client, job, or contract project where their employment status is temporary. For example, a data entry worker employed by a staffing agency and working on a three-month assignment is a temporary worker.

5. Freelance Business Owners

(5%/2.5 million)—Freelancer business owners have one or more employees and consider themselves both a freelancer and a business owner. For example, a social marketing guru who hires a team of other social marketers to build a small agency but still identifies as a freelancer is a freelance business owner.

In some large companies a consultant is referred to as a **vendor**. This is often because they are employees of an approved supplier/provider a company uses.

Large corporations typically have formal supplier programs that manage a list of **approved suppliers and/or providers.** The providers must meet contractual obligations to be approved and maintain a working relationship with the corporation.

I use **agency** in the book as a catch-all term, but qualify it depending on whether I'm referring to large executive management or consulting agencies; marketing, advertising, or public relations agencies; or most often, talent and specialized talent agencies.

SPEED (see Chaps. 3 and 4) is a talent strategy that enables managers to build flexible, project-based teams that get results. It provides a flexible framework for on-demand teams and the ability to adapt to unanticipated business changes by employing five elements: **S**uccess, **P**lan, **E**xecute, **E**valuate, and **D**ecide.

Note: Company names and the people mentioned have been changed in this book.

Don't Have a Kodak Moment

By 2020, 40% of the workforce won't want to be a full-time employee. You can avoid having the infamous "Kodak moment"—when Kodak failed to see the impending disruption to the photography industry by the rise of digital technology—by understanding what the workplace and talent shift means for your business.

Forget the old recruit-and-search-for-months methods for acquiring talent and the perception that "talent" is only full-time employees.

This is why I wrote this book. To show you how to successfully navigate the talent shift that's underway.

Notes

1. "Millennials," Pew Research Center: http://www.pewresearch.org/topics/millennials/. Retrieved Nov. 4, 2015.
2. Joel Kotkin, "The Rise of the 1099 Economy: More Americans Are Becoming Their Own Bosses," *Forbes*, July 25, 2012. Retrieved from http://www.forbes.com/sites/joel-kotkin/2012/07/25/the-rise-of-the-1099-economy-more-americans-are-becoming-their-own-bosses/
3. From "Freelancing in America," Independent study commissioned by Freelancers Union and Upwork. Released October 1, 2015. p. 6. Study retrievable for download at https://fu-web-storage-prod.s3.amazonaws.com/content/filer_public/59/e7/59e70be1-5730-4db8-919f-1d9b5024f939/survey_2015.pdf

CHAPTER 1

Navigating the Shifts in the On-Demand Workplace

The funny thing is, while I didn't consciously seek consulting out initially, I love what I'm doing and this way of working. It lets me focus on doing the work I enjoy, leaving many of the politics and workplace hassles behind. Now, work is an activity I do, not a necessarily a place I go. It's refreshing and has really reinvigorated my career.

—Samantha D., Project manager/consultant

A great workforce shift is underway, driven by a constantly changing global business environment, a highly competitive marketplace that features hyper-specialization, project-based work, and a talent pool that aspires to—and indeed demands—flexibility. Business cycles have accelerated; there's a frequent need for fresh talent, and continuous "recruiting" has become a big part of every manager's job.

A variety of economic, technological, and cultural factors drives this dynamic shift, but three major trends have converged to shape where we are: the coming of age of Millennials,[1] the Baby Boomers' impact on the workforce, and the trend that will impact about 40% of U.S. workers by 2020, the freelance "1099 economy."[2] These trends gained momentum during the Great Recession and its aftermath, emphasizing that old-school mindsets, talent strategies, and even the definition of talent no longer work.

To illustrate, let's start with a story.

Imagine a CEO from the 80's is transported (by way of magic or time travel, your choice) to modern-day Corporate America. He finds that he's the head of a successful business in his industry, but he doesn't understand this new landscape; he's lost as to how to operate in it. The technology both alarms and confuses him. In a panic, he issues a company-wide memorandum ordering that all work must be done on technology from the '80s, telling himself that since it worked for him in the past, he'll make it work now.

Instead of laptops and smartphones, employees are left to handle daily communications using typewriters or clunky DOS computers that only do basic word processing—on a dark green screen with a blinking green cursor. And instead of cloud storage and officewide networks that make collaboration easy and backup reliable, everything is put on floppy discs that must be traded back and forth if more than one person wants to work on the same file.

Anyone who leaves the office must find a payphone if they need to call in to check their messages, find out why they've been paged (remember pagers? or payphones, for that matter?), or get directions if they have lost their way to a big meeting. If anyone outside the company needs to communicate information, it must come in via fax, mail, or courier. When someone needs to look up basic information, it's time to head to the library and the microfiche machine.

How long do you think this business would remain successful? How well do you think any of its employees would be able to do their jobs, even if they were well-regarded hotshots in their industry?

Yes, this is a ridiculous scenario. I've made it as extreme and far-fetched as possible to illustrate the point that *the best and most successful companies, leaders, and managers must evolve and adapt with the times.* They recognize when their "time-tested" strategies, business models, and "best practices" have become outdated or insufficient, and they're willing to invest the time to learn what it takes to stay relevant and competitive in the current landscape.

Consider the case of Borders, the 40-year-old behemoth bookseller that seemed to disappear in an instant in 2011.[3] Why? It was too slow to recognize the changing market and could not, or would not, cannibalize its business to survive, because it didn't understand, or refused to acknowledge, the disruption that was happening. It embraced the Web much too late, did not foresee the rise of eBooks, was too deep in debt, and had opened too many brick-and-mortar stores. What ultimately lead to the company's demise was that its leaders refused to consider changing their business model.

Another story of a company that either ignored the changing market or did not have the talent in place to innovate and survive is the well-documented and rapid demise of Blockbuster.[4] It's a cautionary tale that few businesses saw coming, and certainly not the executives at Blockbuster. At its peak in 2004, Blockbuster had nearly 60,000 employees and more than 9000 stores.[5] With that kind of scale it's easy to think you're impregnable, or perhaps "too big to fail." But the seeds of its fall were planted in 2000 when a fledgling, scrappy company called Netflix proposed a partnership. Its idea: Netflix would run the Blockbuster brand online and Blockbuster would promote Netflix in its stores. Netflix founder Reed Hastings was laughed out of the room.

The rest, as they say, is history, and a pretty ugly one at that for Blockbuster. The company went bankrupt in 2010, and Netflix is now a $28 billion dollar company, about ten times more than what Blockbuster was worth at its peak. The Blockbuster brand is gone—it was a victim of extreme overconfidence and an inability to cope with Netflix's "disruptive innovation."[6]

Whole businesses can disappear seemingly overnight, and new ones launch and transform an industry almost as quickly. In the Blockbuster case, the company had its team in place and a dominant market position—why not go on autopilot and take a vacation, right? Why worry about a pesky online start-up with an outrageous proposal?

Blockbuster missed a massive opportunity, and a huge trend, based in large part on its failure to recognize and appraise the start-up, its ideas, and the talent in its marketplace.

No real company would last, let alone be successful, for more than a week operating by such antiquated methods as those utilized by the CEO from the 1980s scenario. And no employee in that company, no matter how talented he or she might be, would have any real chance of doing work that matters while handicapped by antiquated and ineffective systems.

As with the stories of Borders and Blockbuster, these companies—and your company—cannot afford to miss the signs of a significant business shift similar to the workplace and talent shift that is gaining momentum. How will it impact your business if 40% of available talent will not want to be your employee by 2020? This is one of the many changes underway that businesses are ill-prepared for. I often hear managers lament, "Our recruiters don't understand my business," or "I'm waiting on leadership to approve headcount, which could be months," or "I need to shuffle the people I have on my team instead of building the team I want."

How do companies achieve the goals they need to stay competitive? To do that you need to the right people, but it's no longer feasible to do this in the same ways companies have traditionally used: hiring after you put out a job description, have a recruiter search and interview candidates for eight months, and then finally bring somebody on board under a time line that might take a full year. Even shortening the process to six months is too long. That hiring model is dead; companies simply can no longer survive by using that model.

The best practices of 15, 10, or even 5 years ago no longer apply, yet the way talent is accessed hasn't changed significantly in order to keep pace. As a result, managers are more over-worked and stressed than ever, and their companies are missing out on multimillion-dollar opportunities. Why take months to bring on skilled talent when you need them tomorrow? Why hire generalists when what you really need are skilled special-ists with current-market know-how? Why restrict yourself to a limited talent pool as you struggle to find the right people?

And using those ineffective strategies can be costly.

Severance payments are often a big cost of failing to account for the disruptive and fluctuating realities of the marketplace, especially for larger corporations with large employee rosters. When companies build a mammoth workforce that doesn't have built-in fluidity or adaptability, it's challenging to deal with volatile or unexpected events. They find themselves facing the unenviable task of laying off a large percentage of their workforce when "things happen" in the marketplace, in the economy, or within the business itself.

Take, for instance, the recent examples of tech giants Microsoft and HP, whose hiring decisions on the macro level wound up costing them millions of dollars.

When Microsoft eliminated 18,000 jobs in 2014 shortly after acquiring IT company Nokia, CEO Satya Nadella framed the move in a memo to employees as "realigning their workforce" and "creating the organization and culture to bring their ambi-tions to life." This workforce shift—the largest round of layoffs in company history, affected 15% of Microsoft's employees and cost the company a reported $1.1–$1.6 billion in severance and benefits packages.[7]

HP has gone through similar growing pains. Since 2012, 44,000 employees have been cut as part of HP's master plan to split from one Fortune 50 company into two Fortune 50 companies. It cost the company $1.6 billion in fiscal year 2014 alone, and more layoffs were planned (estimates predict a total of 55,000+ layoffs by the time this shift is over).[8]

Lockheed Martin, the aerospace company and the world's largest defense contractor by sales, disclosed plans in late 2013 to cut 4000 jobs over 18 months as the company restructured its space business and continued its response to uncertainties over domestic and international defense spending.[9] Often Lockheed will have to ramp up its workforce when it wins a contract or ramp down if it loses out on an opportunity. For example, Lockheed laid off nearly 300 people in 2015 after losing the bidding on a contract at the North American Aerospace Defense Command to Raytheon.[10] Another mass layoff occurred in 2011 when the company disclosed plans for a voluntary layoff program affecting 6500 U.S. employees at its corporate headquarters and in its enterprise business services segment. According to Dow Jones, the move was "intended to align its corporate staff with the needs of its businesses." Those decisions brought its job cuts to about 30,000 over a five-year period ending in 2015.[11]

These companies are examples of the constant ebb and flow of a rapidly shifting business environment—and that often involves drastic reductions in headcount.

Managers and executives constantly complain about the "talent shortage." I contend that *there is no talent shortage.*

Many publications reinforce the myth of a talent shortage, such as ManpowerGroup's *2014 Talent Shortage White Paper,*[12] in which 36% of global employers reported that they faced talent shortages in 2014—the highest percentage recorded in seven years.

And according to the Robert Half staffing agency, which produces a quarterly report called *The Demand for Skilled Talent*[13] its first-quarter 2015 report revealed that 49% of employers surveyed by CareerBuilder.com believed "job-specific skills are a scarce commodity," while one in four reported having lost revenue as a result of delays in filling open positions.

The fastest way to drive business results is hiring the right people in the right roles at the right time. As business models and the marketplace change, companies need the ability to adapt and acquire new skills in order to stay competitive. As a result, talent has become a competitive advantage.

An abundance of amazingly talented people are ready to fill your open positions. The challenge is an inability to find and connect with this talent.

Fortunately, unlike a talent shortage, which could take years to overcome as companies wait for new talent to graduate into the marketplace and acquire the experience needed, this employer/talent disconnect is an issue that can be fixed, and fixed rapidly. How? By changing your perception of talent, you'll see there is an untapped pool of highly specialized consultants—experts in their specific discipline with core competencies perfectly suited to fill the talent gaps faced by businesses small and large. These experts are focused on creating the biggest impact for you in the fastest timeframe possible because that's all that they'll be doing.[14]

The right experts are people who have done the work and have *mastery* over the subject. They've been there, done that, and learned from experience. They can adapt to changes, overcome obstacles, and generate solutions on the spot because they've seen it all. I call them "real-world experts" because they have the in-the-trenches experience needed to jump in and immediately make an impact. Companies often lack the time to train people and need them to hit the ground running.

The great thing about flexible, highly specialized talent is that they're "plug and play" ready. They have the industry knowledge and they know the vernacular. Whatever your project, whatever gap you need to bridge between the skills your current employees possess and the skills needed to address your latest challenge, this talent is poised and ready to get the job done, and done right.

As the founder and CEO of Simplicity Consulting, I am in contact with thousands of people who are experienced, able, and eager to work. These people tell me things like, "I want to make an impact and do the work I love for a company that values and appreciates my experience." A vast amount of talent is out there, and they're looking for the right opportunities. The problem is that the project roles and the talent aren't finding each other quickly and efficiently.

Therein resides the true problem. Like the single people who complain there's no one out there for them, when in reality they've been looking in all the wrong places, something is amiss with the way managers and executives are attempting to find the talent they need. What's seen as a "gap" is actually a result of misperceptions about the available talent, and also using inadequate and inefficient talent acquisition methods.

Whatever your job is and whatever position you have in an organization, whether big or small, whether you're in finance, marketing, sales, product development, or engineering, you are constantly evaluating how your role is helping to grow the company, and how to do it in the most efficient way possible. This applies directly to the people you bring in. More specifically, ask them exactly what the work is that they're delivering and make sure that it adds value to the organization's goals.

In a world where the latest smartphone is obsolete almost the instant you buy it, managers and their companies need every resource and tool at their disposal to stay relevant, competitive, and ahead of the curve. They also must recognize when times have changed (which can happen overnight) and be willing and prepared to change—even if that means letting go of "the way things have always been done" and learning a way to do them better.

When it comes to finding the right talent—one of the most precious resources any company has—many managers are just as handicapped as our hypothetical workers with the CEO from the past.

There are a number of factors behind this. Busy managers are asked to do more with less and secure the ideal team when they often aren't even clear on the specific nuances of the positions they are trying to fill, let alone the overarching implications for the business's long-term needs.

Finally, more and more of today's companies face project-based challenges. They need specialists who can address a specific project need or meet a specific goal, and traditional talent acquisition methods don't allow for this sort of specialization and flexibility. The old method of placing butts in seats doesn't cut it any more. There are other problems and issues: how do I stay ahead of my competition? How am I attracting not only the best talent but also the right talent for what we need?

To succeed in this environment, organizational agility is the key. Think about the Borders and Blockbuster experiences. Having a mindset that restricts you to a team of only FTEs is no longer an option for businesses that want to remain relevant.

To hire fast and hire right, employers will need to embrace a broader definition of talent and create flexible, project-based teams. By widening their vision, they will tap into a much larger pool of available talent and find the smart, creative people they need for each project—regardless of whether these people are consultants, contractors, "supertemps," freelancers, self-employed, retirees, full-time employees (FTEs), or whatever title they use.

Navigating the Talent Shift will show you how to tap into a broad talent pool of freelancers and consultants to build the on-demand teams you need in a project-based environment. You will learn how these on-demand teams get results by moving more nimbly, faster, and smarter than ever.

Have you tapped into the Baby Boomer talent pool? As freelancers and consultants, they are among the most experienced, and they are eager to put their expertise to work to mentor others and to add value to projects. The generation that has redefined everything as they move through their lives, the Baby Boomers are not embracing their parents' idea of retirement for economic, lifestyle, and professional reasons.

In Chap. 2 you will meet Reese and Daniel. They are part of the Millennial generation that comprised the 54 million adult Americans in 2015. That's one-third of the American workforce, the largest generation at work, according to a June 23, 2015, *Fortune* article that cites Pew Research Center statistics.[15] Millennials want more work choice and control in their lives, and those drivers are major components of the shift to the on-demand, project-based workplace.

I've seen how agility and outside-the-box thinking enabled some organizations to stay competitive and drive innovation in impressive ways, accelerating their business results and allowing them to move nimbly in response to the turbulent marketplace.

Those companies look at talent acquisition in a different way; for one thing, it's highly *project-oriented*. They assemble the right team for a project's needs using a customized mix of full-time employees, consultants, and/or independent experts in order to solve talent problems *right now.* Companies are creating teams of experts for short- and long-term projects in order to deliver high-impact results. You'll meet some of these companies later in this book.

I've seen the emergence of the project-based workplace. Clients are focusing on their business through a project lens: they're looking at their goals as projects. These could be long-term projects; they could be strategic projects; they could be tactical projects. It's really about identifying the right talent resources for specific kinds of projects.

It's time to acquire the people you need by accessing a much broader talent pool. It's time to have a team of on-demand experts whenever you need them and for as long or short a period of time as will make your projects successful.

In my work with leading companies, I've observed that most managers have the same aspirations: they want to do big things, to make an impact, to achieve their goals efficiently while remaining nimble and flexible. They share similar challenges on how to continuously evolve their teams and adapt to market changes in a fluid and effective way.

Unfortunately many are just as stuck as our time-traveling CEO in the story—with a mindset and a talent strategy from another era. It's time to have a talent strategy that takes into account the talent shift underway.

In this book, you will learn:

- How a proven on-demand talent acquisition strategy will get results
- Why having access to a broader talent pool is vital

- How to build and integrate on-demand teams in a project-based world
- How to be nimble and flexible when you need to access and acquire talent
- Why the "loyalty question" is not an issue
- How you pay someone doesn't change the relationship or value of the work
- About the top strategies and best practices from managers who have overcome common roadblocks

I'll show you how you can build on-demand teams that are fast and flexible, and most importantly, will enable your business to grow.

Notes

1. "Millennials," Pew Research Center: http://www.pewresearch. org/topics/millennials/ Retrieved Nov. 4, 2015
2. Joel Kotkin, "The Rise of the 1099 Economy: More Americans Are Becoming Their Own Bosses," *Forbes*, July 25, 2012. Retrieved from http://www.forbes.com/sites/joelkotkin/2012/07/25/the-rise-of-the-1099-economy-more-americans-are-becoming-their-own-bosses/
3. Josh Sanburn, "5 Reasons Borders Went of Business (and What Will Take its Place)," *Time,* July 19, 2011. Retrieved November 17, 2015, from http://business.time.com/2011/07/19/5-reasons-borders-went-out-of-business-and-what-will-take-its-place/
4. Greg Satell, "A Look Back at Why Blockbuster Really Failed and Why It Didn't Have To," *Forbes*, September 5, 2014. Retrieved from http://www.forbes.com/sites/gregsatell/2014/09/05/a-look-back-at-why-blockbuster-really-failed-and-why-it-didnt-have-to/
5. "A Timeline: The Blockbuster Life Cycle," *Forbes*, April 7, 2011. Retrieved from http://www.forbes.com/2010/05/18/blockbuster-netflix-coinstar-markets-bankruptcy-coinstar_slide.html
6. "What Is Disruptive Innovation?" *DigitalTonto*, August 23, 2009. Retrieved from http://www.digitaltonto.com/2009/what-is-disruptive-innovation/

7. Nick Wingfield, "Microsoft to Lay Off Thousands, Most from Nokia Unit." *New York Times*, July 17, 2014. Retrieved from http://www.nytimes.com/2014/07/18/business/microsoft-to-cut-up-to-18000-jobs.html?_r=0

8. Julie Bort, "Meg Whitman Again Hints That HP Will Lay Off More Workers As It Splits in Two," "HP Will Spend about $2 Billion for Its 'Unprecedented' Separation into two Fortune 50 Companies," *Business Insider*, February 24 and June 3, 2015. Retrieved from http://www.businessinsider.com/meg-whitman-hints-at-more-layoffs-again-2015-6 and http://www.businessinsider.com/hp-separation-will-cost-about-2-billion-2015-2

9. Doug Cameron and Ben Fox Rubin, "Lockheed Martin to Cut 4,000 Jobs, Close Sites," *Wall Street Journal*, November 14, 2013. Retrieved from http://www.wsj.com/articles/SB10001424052702303289904579197643781636608

10. George Leopold, "Lockheed Martin Begins Layoffs at NORAD," *Defense Systems,* July 30, 2015. Retrieved from https://defensesystems.com/articles/2015/07/30/lockheed-norad-isc2-layoffs.aspx

11. "Lockheed Martin Sets Voluntary Layoff Plan for 6,500 Employees" *MarketWatch*, July 19, 2011. Retrieved from http://www.advfn.com/nyse/StockNews.asp?stocknews=LMT&article=48498790

12. "The Talent Shortage Continues," Manpower Group Slideshare from the 2014 Talent Shortage White Paper. Retrieved October 6, 2015, from http://www.slideshare.net/ExperisCH/2014-talent-shortage-white-paper

13. "The Demand for Skilled Talent," *Robert Half.* Retrieved October 6, 2015, from http://www.roberthalf.com/workplace-research/the-demand-for-skilled-talent

14. Jody Greenstone Miller and Matt Miller, "The Rise of the Supertemp," *Harvard Business Review,* May 2012. Retrieved November 12, 2015, at https://hbr.org/2012/05/the-rise-of-the-supertemp

15. Katherine Reynolds Lewis, "Everything You Need to Know about Your Millennial Co-workers," *Fortune*, June 23, 2015. Retrieved from http://fortune.com/2015/06/23/know-your-millennial-co-workers/

CHAPTER 2

The Changing Face of Talent

*M*any of us grew up with parents that worked the same job for 30 years. That paradigm has shifted, and while consulting may seem unstable, it is really not that much different than being an employee. Reorganizations happen and roles go away. Being a consultant, **I feel more in control of my destiny to choose the roles that are right for me.**

—Hannah M., *Readiness Program Manager*

In Chap. 1, I covered three major trends that have converged to make up the talent shift, but if you look into the generational impacts of the Baby Boomers, Millennials, and the large free-lance workforce, the primary commonalities are control and choice.

Control and choice are the keywords of the freelancers and consultants who compose this evolutionary and revolutionary change, as noted by many including Dan Pink[1] and the *Harvard Business Review*.[2] And the numbers of freelancers are huge.

Forbes[3] has reported that "the Bureau of Labor and Statistics estimates that by 2020 as many as 65 million Americans will be freelancers, independent consultants and solopreneurs, making up 40 percent of the workforce." TechCrunch even asserted that "in the future, employees won't exist."[4]

The primary focus of this book is to teach executives and managers how to find and integrate this broad base of freelancers and consultants into their projects. But first you have to understand who these people are and the reasons why choice and control are so paramount in their working lives.

There is no one-size-fits all profile of people choosing to work on-demand; it encompasses all ages, expertise levels, and industries. Let's meet a few of these people.

How a Life Event Inspired Theresa to Take Control over Her Time

"I knew the moment I realized that I could not be with my husband and family at my father-in-law's viewing because I had no vacation time that I had to leave my job. I had to gain control of the priorities in my life."[5]

Theresa, 54, was able to get the time off from her advertising executive job to attend the Jewish funeral but could not get time off to attend the unveiling a few months later.

It was a watershed moment: Theresa realized she had to quit her job. She had missed a lot of important family moments during her career, which she justified by saying, "I will get to the next one." But she realized that with a funeral there was no "next one." So she became a freelance editor and hasn't looked back. The benefits of having control of her time and being able to place her family at the same level of importance as her professional work have continued to suit her life even more now that she's a grandmother of two.

Since embarking on this new path, her long-term business relationships include clients ranging from start-ups to established companies. Her clients know she'll get the work done when they need it. And she does, but sometimes it gets done in the early morning or late evenings if she's taking care of her one year-old granddaughter, Hazel, or attending a local event with friends. A few months ago her daughter landed her first job as a special needs teacher and needed to set up a regular classroom for special needs kids. Theresa was able to step in and devote two days to painting blackboards, peeling away old posters, and getting the special needs classroom ready. It gave her immense pleasure to block out the time she needed to help her daughter—and indirectly her daughter's young students. Theresa didn't have to file a request to get the time off to do it.

"I'm a wife, stepmother, mom to two adult twins, a grandmother of two and a very busy editor on some wonderful projects. My priorities are in balance with how I spend my days."

Career Choice: Hard-Wired to Create on Her Own Terms

When Reese, now 25, was 12 years old and coding on Neopets,[6] she did not dream that one day she'd become a software engineer. After graduating from a six-month intensive engineering bootcamp, she landed a job at a top event ticketing company. Reese is a full-time employee (FTE) and has less than one year on the job. She enjoys her first experience in corporate America, but flexibility and a healthy work/life balance is a long-term priority for her. She takes a day to work remotely whenever she needs it, but for now she does enjoy the camaraderie and face-to-face collaboration at her employee-centric San Francisco office. Down the road, she envisions that she'll work three to four days from home or from wherever it suits her.

When she has a family, she wants to work on dynamic engineering projects and devote the time she wants to her family—either by working with multiple companies on a project basis, starting her own company, or creating apps.[7] While she is very happy in her current FTE role, when she started her career she knew that choice and control were hers to make.

Jumping off the Corporate Treadmill, but Keeping Her Feet Firmly Planted With Flexibility and Challenging Work

When Keri's daughter was born, she stepped away from the corporate world, including working for some major consumer product and technology companies, and decided to provide marketing and public relations services on a freelance basis. She did so with no idea what the demand would be but has since found it exciting and challenging. The ability to do interesting work gives her a sense of fulfillment and engagement, particularly because the majority of it has been with start-ups and non-profits.

Going out on her own was a bit scary—particularly because of the loss of 401K benefits and the addition of the self-employment taxes. But she has the ability to evaluate each project and say, "That project doesn't look exciting, or that person is someone I really don't want to work with, so I'm not going to do it."[8]

Even though she is working from home, she says she is challenged in the same way she was when working for large companies, but a big difference is that she can use her skills to help a company that truly needs her.

Keri has found the right balance between challenging projects and flexibility. "The project I'm working on now is really challenging," she said. "I have a natural drive to take on challenging projects. But later on if I decide I don't want to do it anymore, I can tell my client that I'll find them somebody who matches my skills and go on and just do something else that feels good to me."

Exercising the Expert and Creative Muscles

Daniel, 25, came to consulting work as a result of a number of circumstances that made it difficult for him to get a job in the field he had focused on in college. He was able to improvise by doing consulting work.

Consulting gives him the autonomy and the ability to "do very well with limited direction and the opportunity to exercise that creative muscle," he said. It also allowed him to work in an environment where he is trusted to meet a deadline and figure out the best and most creative way to get a project done, without the interruptions of constant updates, reporting, or oversight.

He said that he is treated with a different and higher level of respect than is true of many of his peers in FTE positions. He believes that his autonomy and independence are both celebrated and appreciated. Rather than the "very hands on, breathes-down-your-neck" type of management style that he feels is all too present in traditional positions (and even in his previous consulting position), he is able to work at his own pace.

Though he appreciates the autonomy and the opportunity to work on high-value projects, he recognizes that there are risks. For example, one risk is the sacrifice of the kind of stability that comes with a full-time job. Daniel recognizes the value and freedom that comes with consulting, but he also likes to take a "hybrid" approach, where part of his time is spent working remotely and part is on site, as he believes that there is a huge value "in going in and being around other people." Otherwise, he says, "You might operate in a silo and sometimes it's difficult to be motivated."

The Swiss Army Knife: Variety Has Its Own Rewards

Samantha, 45, had worked for a large corporation for eight years when she was laid off during a round of downsizing. She immediately reached out to the extended network that she had built through the years and connected with a manager who was about to begin work on an "incubation business" that had so many needs it was described to Samantha in this way: "I don't know what I don't know. Can you come in for a month and help me identify what kinds of things we should be focusing on and how things are going?"

Thus began a new career as an expert "Swiss Army Knife." The promise of a month's worth of work turned into an "open-ended engagement," during which Samantha had multiple opportunities "to grow the business and target new audiences." The one-month trial turned into six months, then another six months, and has lasted more than five years.

Samantha uses her expertise wherever her manager knows help is needed most, though sometimes she is working on projects that the manager herself needs help with. "She also basically volunteers me for anyone else on her leadership team wherever they need help."

> "I end up playing this really diverse role on the team.... [the manager] would have to hire four or five different people as full-time employees to do all the different things that I cover. She doesn't need four or five employees and all that overhead—nor does she have the headcount to do that. I'm a very nimble resource who has subject matter expertise in a number of different areas. She and her team can deploy me wherever and whenever they need me."

Samantha says that there are many occasions when she is asked why her manager doesn't simply hire her as a full-time employee—to which she responds that there isn't a job description at the company that covers what she does. She says that there are so many things that she is able to provide that she has earned a reputation as somebody who simply "gets stuff done." She notes that she has "actually been around and on teams longer than most people who are full-time employees."

Referring to her unique position as a consultant working with the same team for such a long period of time, she says, "I like having both a long-term engagement and relationship. It's just how I prefer to work from a perspective of continuity and getting to know people and not constantly looking for something new to work on, which is often a big part of what some consultants face when they do more target-based work."

What Talent Wants

As you can see from the above stories, on-demand talent works in different industries and companies and takes on many roles. It's not one type of individual; rather it's how they perceive choice and control. They also want flexibility, high-value work, autonomy and respect, and to make a difference.

Flexibility

As Hannah said at the start of this chapter, she wanted more control of her destiny and the ability to "choose the roles that are right for me."

Talent doesn't need a watershed moment like Theresa's story to gain control over their schedules and lives.

The stories above share a common thread—the need for flexibility and balance in their working lives, items that can be hard if not impossible to find in a traditionally structured job. People want fulfilling and challenging work that also gives them the freedom to spend time with their families and explore their personal passions. They want working arrangements that work *with* their lives rather than against them. They don't want to be squeezed into a box that puts the rest of their lives on hold and forces them to cram anything not labelled "work" into evenings and weekends.

The professional services firm EY substantiated this concept when it released findings from a 2015 global survey[9] about the work-life challenges employees confront. One of the main takeaways was that, in the United States, Millennials want flexible work arrangements—and that they will relocate to gain flexibility. The survey added that Millennials worry about "flexibility stigma"—the likelihood that they'll be labeled as less than fully committed, or "loyal," if they use arrangements like flextime and paternity leave—and as a result suffer negative job and career consequences.

Demonstrating a corporate disconnect with employee interest in working flexibly, the EY research found that in the U.S. nearly one in ten (9%) workers overall say they have "suffered a negative consequence as a result of having a flexible work schedule," and the rate is even higher for Millennials—nearly one in six (15%). Negative consequences include losing a job, being denied a promotion or raise, being assigned to less interesting or high-profile assignments, or being publicly or privately reprimanded.[10]

The EY survey also found that 48% of Millennials who are parents are much more likely to take paid parental leave compared to parents of older generations when they had children (Gen X 35% and boomers 24%). In addition, they appear to value increased flexibility and paid parental leave more than other generations and are more likely to have made, or be willing to make, sacrifices to manage work and family/personal responsibilities. For example, U.S. Millennials are the most likely generation to say they would change jobs (77%) or careers (76%), give up an opportunity for a promotion (65%), or "move my family to another location" (66%). They would also be more willing to move closer to family (62%) and to "take a pay cut to have flexibility" (44%).[11]

Big corporations, including Netflix, Virgin, Johnson & Johnson, and Microsoft, are paying attention to parental leave trends illustrated by the EY survey. They have made sweeping changes to support employees and their families by offering more paid leave for new parents. President Barrack Obama also took steps to increase access to paid sick leave[12] for government employees, and has called for a national paid leave law.

These are just a few examples of a growing movement in the United States. Companies are recognizing the importance of creating a flexible company culture that makes talent feel supported and valued.

High-Value Work/Problem Solving

In addition to flexibility, consultants want to do high-value work; they are there to solve problems by using their "intellectual capital,"[13] as Peter Drucker put it, and their experience.

"We don't compete. I want to help you show up better and do great work," says Samantha to her FTE team members. She has crafted a career as a "Swiss Army Knife"—the person with the tools who can tackle just about any project, even the most difficult, and make it a success.

Consultants want to imbue teams with the problem-solving spirit: "You have to really empower people to let them help you solve the problem," says Diana, whose story is featured in Chap. 8.

Deborah, a management consultant, said she likes projects "where I can be empowered to really 'run' things and have input. I really enjoy projects where I am a respected member of a group." She emphasized the importance of "feeling valued" and "being allowed to really have fun with a project while working in a culture that is supportive and values consultants."[14]

Because they have chosen the projects they work on, and because the company has chosen them, bringing value is core to the consultant's purpose. Simply put, it's what they do and what drives them.

Autonomy and Respect

While some companies are embracing progressive ideas like flexible work schedules and working remotely, for many people, seeking true autonomy in their work means leaving the world of FTEs altogether and embarking on a career as a consultant, freelancer, or other alternative role.

Independence and the ability to work at his own pace is an important aspect of project work for Daniel. Rather than having to waste time answering to several managers about the same project at the cost of actually working, he is trusted to meet deadlines and get the job done.

And there's a certain amount of respect, especially for younger consultants, that comes when companies allow remote work. "I think that's a huge perk," he says. "I find very frequently that I can spend some extra time on deliverables when I need to if I'm not worrying about that commute."

Samantha prefers her role as a "power contractor" rather than being a full-time employee because of the added benefits, including flexibility and avoiding the internal pressures that come from reporting to a manager, being reviewed or meeting certain expectations. "The hours I work and whether I work on weekends or evenings—that's kind of up to me."

"I take my daughter to school and take time off when I want," says Fred Talmadge, a freelance software and app developer. "When I was still at my traditional job, I dreamt of working on my own, and freelancing online has provided me that opportunity. I do not have any intentions to go back to a traditional job."[15]

Consultants like to stretch, grow, and further develop their skills, and they like projects that provide them with the opportunity to do that. They look upon project-based work as opportunities to gain respect, increase their knowledge, and share what they learn with current and future colleagues.

To Make a Difference

"I was raised to believe I could change the world. I'm desperate for you to show me that the work we do here matters, even just a little bit. I'll make copies, I'll fetch coffee, I'll do the grunt work. But I'm not going to help you get a new Mercedes," says Elizabeth McLeod, a Millennial and cum laude graduate of Boston University.[16]

"I'll give you everything I've got, but I need to know it makes a difference to something bigger than your bottom line."[17]

More and more people, across all ages and experience levels, want to do high-impact work in a way that makes the most sense for their lifestyles, and delivering real value to companies they feel a sense of connection to. Sometimes this can happen in a traditional corporate job, but there are many other ways to deliver impact and find meaning in your career.

Hannah says she looks for projects where she "can really dig in, solve problems and make a difference. When I hear about a role and get excited, that is the right role for me."

"People are increasingly building flexible careers on their own terms, based on their passions, desired lifestyle and access to a much broader pool of opportunities than ever before in history," said Stephane Kasriel, CEO of Upwork. "While we are still relatively early in the rise of the freelance workforce, there's no doubt its growth will continue. Professionals are not only turning away from traditional employment, once they do most have no desire to go back."[18]

A joint survey[19] conducted by the Freelancers Union and Upwork in late 2015 underscored Kasriel's statement. The survey found that the independent, freelance workforce in America was nearly 54 million people in late 2015, more than one-third of the entire U.S. workforce.

This puts the talent shift I'm talking about in sharp perspective and underscores its importance to the future of business and the U.S. economy. In addition, the study, the second done by Upwork and the Freelancers Union, said that the freelance workforce increased by about 700,000 over the total tracked in 2014.

Other survey findings included:

- The majority (60%) of freelancers who left traditional employment now earn more than they did as FTEs.
- Almost one in four (23%) said they quit a job with an employer in order to freelance. Of those who earn more, 78% indicated they earned more freelancing within a year or less.
- Freelancing is seen as a positive step not only for professionals but also for the economy; more than one-third of freelancers report that demand for their services increased in the past year, and nearly half expected their income from freelancing to increase in the coming year.
- Technology is making it easier to find freelance work (73% of freelancers agree compared to 69% in 2014)—3 in 4 non-freelancers are open to doing additional work outside their primary jobs to earn more money, if it was available. More than half (51%) of

the freelancers had obtained a project online, up from 42% in 2014.

- Flexibility is the top reason people choose to freelance full time.
- When asked why they freelance, people freelancing full time cited as major reasons freedom over when and where they work, being their own boss, and pursuit of work they are passionate about.
- Freelancers, especially Millennials, are optimistic about the outlook for freelancing.
- 50% of freelancers said they would not quit freelancing and take a traditional job with an employer—no matter how much it paid.

People have more choices than ever before to move sideways, backwards, forwards, or even pause. Careers are more lattice[20] than ladder or even a jungle gym. People might moonlight from their regular jobs or work part time for one or more companies. Project-based work, which provides more flexibility than a traditional corporate jobs, is one way many people choose to move across their career lattices. This is a fairly recent development, especially for different segments of the workforce.

For instance, the old "work for one business till you retire" mentality is no longer realistic, or even feasible, for the modern workplace. That model is a thing of the past. The business environment is shifting too rapidly, and talent is adapting accordingly in order to survive by the rules of the new game.

Baby Boomers (people born between 1946 and the early '60s) and GenXers (those born from the early '60s to the early '80s) started off their careers with the mindset of working for one company for the long haul. However, many have learned that their dedication to one or two employers no longer pays off for them the way it did for their parents and grandparents.

According to a study by MBO Partners reported on MarketWatch.com,[21] nearly 5 million Baby Boomers "have decided to go it alone into the world of business and work as 'solopreneurs.' But these are not workers who have been set adrift by traditional employers with few other options besides self-employment. More than half of them chose to be independent, new research shows."

The boomers surveyed in the MBO Partners[22] study, for instance, gave the following as reasons why they enjoy being consultants:

- They like being challenged and motivated (6%).
- They like making an impact (56%).
- They like being their own boss (60%).
- For many, flexibility (79%) and doing what they like (77%) are more important than money.

Generation X is the third major part of the workforce. There are 65 million Gen Xers compared to 77 million Baby Boomers and 83 million Millennials. I often say Generation X is the "sandwich generation" because we—I can say "we" because I am one—are sandwiched between the Baby Boomers and the Millennials. In general, Gen Xers have seen their parents have long careers, typically with one company that included pensions, security, and retirement. Upon entering the workforce, I've seen many Gen Xers approach work in much the same way. And then business shifted, hitting Gen Xers harder because of their positions in middle and upper management, forcing millions of Gen Xers to redefine how they think about their careers. They thought they were doing the right thing, doing what they were told, but then some found themselves with a severance package.

Meanwhile, Millennials, as in the stories above, are proving that professionals have more choices than ever before and are choosing to work in the way that best suits their lifestyle for whatever stage of their career they are in. Born between the early '80s and the early 2000s, they are the newest entrants into the workforce. Millennials increasingly demand a different kind of career path from the get-go. They don't see themselves as attached to a specific company so much as to a specific mission or purpose. They eschew the corporate, 9-to-5 structure and instead focus on adding value and doing meaningful work on their own terms. According to a recent article on Inc.com,[23] over one-third of Millennials think of themselves as freelancers and 32% anticipate working more flexible hours in years to come. Forbes reports that 60% of these workers plan to leave their corporate jobs in three years or less.[24]

Sara Horowitz writes that Millennials "understand the future of work better than anyone else."[25]Millennials intuitively understand that the "9-5 grind" is not the future. "They are, in a sense, the first generation of freelance natives. They're embracing freelancing in a way no other generation has. And now, they're the majority of the workforce." The Internet, she continues, "has opened more doors to this generation than any other," with nearly 40% of them freelancing compared to 32% of all other groups.

The days of businesses building empires of FTEs are over. The multi-generational groups of freelancers, experts, and consultants that will compose 40% of the workforce by 2020 is available to you on-demand. This talent pool is too large to ignore. It's time for a new talent strategy. The next two chapters introduce and describe SPEED™, the talent strategy that enables you to build flexible, project-based teams that get results.

Notes

1. Dan Pink is the author of five books, including *Drive: The Surprising Truth about What Motivates Us* (2009) and *Free Agent Nation: The Future of Working for Yourself* (2001). See his website: http://www.danpink.com/about/
2. Clayton M. Christensen, Dina Wang, Derek van Bever, "Consulting on the Cusp of Disruption," *Harvard Business Review*. October 2013. Article retrieved November 12, 2015, at https://hbr.org/2013/10/consulting-on-the-cusp-of-disruption
3. Adriana Lopez, "Coworking Is It Just a Fad or the Future of Business," *Forbes Online*, April 25, 2013. Available at http://www.forbes.com/sites/adrianalopez/2013/04/25/coworking-is-it-just-a-fad-or-the-future-of-business/
4. Tad Milbourn, "In the Future, Employees Won't Exist," *TechCrunch*, June 13, 2015. Available at http://techcrunch.com/2015/06/13/in-the-future-employees-wont-exist/

5. October 2014 interview.

6. Neopets is a virtual pet website: http://www.neopets.com/

7. Interview on October 5, 2015.

8. Interview November, 2015.

9. "Global Generations," a study conducted online by Harris Poll on behalf of EY within the U.S. between November 2014 and January 14, 2015. Available for download at http://www.ey.com/US/en/About-us/Our-people-and-culture/EY-work-life-challenges-across-generations-global-study

10. Ibid.

11. Ibid.

12. Gretchen Gavett, "Who Has Paid Sick Leave, Who Doesn't, and What's Changing," *Harvard Business Review*, January 21, 2015. Retrieved from https://hbr.org/2015/01/who-has-paid-sick-leave-who-doesnt-and-whats-changing

13. Peter F. Drucker, "The New Productivity Challenge," *Harvard Business Review*, November–December 1991. Retrieved November 12, 2015, at https://hbr.org/1991/11/the-new-productivity-challenge/ar/1

14. Response to email questions, March 2015.

15. Quoted in "Freelancing in America: 2015," *a* study released on October 1, 2015, by the Freelancers Union and Upwork. Study retrievable for download at https://fu-web-storage-prod.s3.amazonaws.com/content/filer_public/59/e7/59e70be1-5730-4db8-919f-1d9b5024f939/survey_2015.pd

16. "Why Millennials Keep Dumping You: An Open Letter to Management," LinkedIn Pulse, October 3, 2015. Retrieved from https://www.linkedin.com/pulse/why-millennials-keep-dumping-you-open-letter-lisa-earle-mcleod

17. Ibid.

18. Quoted in "Freelancing in America: 2015," Press release, October 1, 2015, by the Freelancers Union and Upwork. Retrieved from https://www.upwork.com/press/2015/10/01/freelancers-union-and-upwork-release-new-study-revealing-insights-into-the-almost-54-million-people-freelancing-in-america/

19. "Freelancing in America," Independent study commissioned by Freelancers Union and Upwork. Released October 1, 2015. Study retrievable for download at https://fu-web-storage-prod. s3.amazonaws.com/content/filer_public/59/e7/59e70be1-5730-4db8-919f-1d9b5024f939/survey_2015.pdf

20. Cathy Benko, Molly Anderson, and Suzanne Vickberg, "The Corporate Lattice," *Deloitte University Press*, January 1, 2011. Retrieved October 6, 2015, from http://dupress.com/articles/the-corporate-lattice-rethinking-careers-in-the-changing-world-of-work/

21. "MBO Partners Highlight Key Characteristics of Independent Workers in the On-Demand Economy," *MarketWatch*, April 21, 2015. Retrieved November 9, 2015, at http://www.marketwatch.com/story/mbo-partners-highlight-key-characteristics-of-independent-workers-in-the-on-demand-economy-2015-04-21

22. Ibid.

23. Tess Townsend, "Survey: Workforce Is Going to the Freelancers," Inc., Nov. 1, 2015. Retrieved Nov. 12, 2015, at http://www.inc.com/tess-townsend/freelancing-in-america-2015-survey.html

24. Kate Taylor, "Why Millennials Are Ending The 9 To 5," *Forbes*, August 23, 2015. Retrieved from http://www.forbes.com/sites/katetaylor/2013/08/23/why-millennials-are-ending-the-9-to-5/

25. Sara Horowitz, "Why Millennials Understand the Future of Work Better Than Anyone Else," *Fast Company*, April 1, 2015. Retrieved October 6, 2015, from http://www.fastcompany.com/3044478/the-future-of-work/why-millennials-understand-the-future-of-work-more-than-anyone-else

CHAPTER 3

The SPEED Solution

*I*t's so fast. I usually can have someone start work within 10 days easily or faster...It's one-tenth of the time it would take to hire someone full-time.

—Amanda F., technology company manager

Michael, like many managers, is in meetings almost every day from 8 a.m. to 6 p.m. and triple-booked much of the time. Michael is a rising star in the company and is highly valued by executives, who often ask him to work on important projects. As a result, everyone wants a piece of him. His team values him as their manager and trusts him to be a great advocate for them. Michael's professional success has opened many doors and new relationships, but has come with a cost—huge burdens on his time and priorities. He runs an important but relatively small team that has many responsibilities. He manages to hold it all together, but barely.

Recently Michael's budget was slashed by 20%, although he is expected to deliver on the same goals with even fewer resources. He is frustrated; if he is such a valuable employee, why is he still expected to deliver the same level and quality of work with fewer resources? Complaining is out of the question because nobody wants to hear problems, only solutions. Unfortunately, that mindset from management won't spur success. Michael's stress is mounting as he works to figure out how to get it all done because, after all, he is a star.

How will Michael handle this dilemma? How will he justify getting more headcount with a 20% cut to his budget? Meanwhile, his normal work still needs to get done, so he's behind and even more panicked about his credibility, which rests on his ability to deliver on key goals.

He needs creative solutions and fast.

Like Michael, I've seen this scenario become common as organizations must deal with changes in their markets and internal resources. Managers try to do their best, but there are challenges.

A Few Challenges

Managers Have to Do More with Less

Managers live and work in a complicated world where job roles, duties, and expectations evolve and the pace quickens. Budgets are set for the year but often must shift as events occur. In addition, many companies are adopting "zero cost budgeting," meaning that every year they start with zero and have to justify their budget needs rather than looking at the previous year's budget and editing it for the current year. Many managers have more tasks added to their responsibilities, but then don't get the funds they need.

With all of that happening, it's difficult to carve out the time needed to reflect on how to define and implement a successful project.

No Time to Specify Your Desired Outcomes

As a result of having to do more with less (while doing it faster), managers often fail to take the time necessary to clearly define the desired outcomes for their projects. What does success look like for this project? How does this project contribute to the company's goals? The answers to these questions will help determine who and what is needed to bring the project to a successful completion.

Desired outcomes also come into play when building your team and interviewing talent. Most managers have a good idea of what they want in a candidate, but they may have a hard time articulating it or putting it into a project description. I've seen some project descriptions that consist of a mere three bullet points, and ones that are long laundry lists of generic skills and responsibilities. I've seen descriptions that say things as vague as, "I need a rock star who can do community management." Okay, "rock star" is a fun term, but what is your definition of a "rock star"? What qualifications does this person have? What will they be expected to do on a day-to-day basis, and what value will they contribute to the business?

Too Many Generalists and Too Few Specialists

In a global business economy, companies need to be able to test ideas and change direction quickly. This is especially challenging if most of your team is made up of generalists, who might not have the specialized skills needed for a new or strategic project. A specialist can be brought in to focus on a new idea or a specific campaign, as opposed to the many items that generalists have on their checklist. Since the specialists aren't buried by multiple projects, they are hyper-focused and will have the most impact on the project in the fastest time possible.

Another benefit is perspective. "Specialists bring a fresh perspective and can help employees examine the direction of the project in a new light," says Matthew, an operations program manager.[1]

The world is full of specialists—experts in their disciplines with core competencies ideally suited to fill the talent gaps faced by small and large businesses. They are the game changers and the innovators; they are also a fairly low-risk solution—if the right specialist is chosen. Accessing them requires an enlightened, comprehensive strategy.

Where Does All This Leave You?

After a decade of working in the trenches to help companies build on-demand teams to achieve their goals and excel, the answer to the above question is to adopt a low-risk, flexible, and faster talent strategy.

"Finding talent is much more fluid, opportunistic and fast-paced," a 2014 article in the *Harvard Business Review* said. "This new structure allows team members to focus on leveraging their unique set of expertise to deliver greater results…It also leaves the old ways of acquiring talent, measuring goals and relating to employees in the dust, because they were designed at a time when business was consistent and static."[2]

Companies increasingly look at their goals and their successes in terms of projects. These might be long-term projects; they might be strategic projects; they might be more tactical projects.

Whatever the case, finding on-demand talent is about identifying the right resources for each specific project, which requires a new strategy conventional approaches lack. Those approaches are seriously out of step with the evolving and fluctuating realities of the on-demand workforce and project-based workplace. Companies need access to a worldwide, on-demand talent pool, or they'll face significant costs to their bottom line. In addition, there is the potential cost to innovation.

Too often managers must deal with how to do their job with less—less staff, less budget, less time. The message for managers? Talent is more empowered than ever to design their career paths—they have more choices when it comes to how, when, and where they work, and for whom they work. And that won't change. If these realities are not included in your strategy, you're missing out on tapping into a growing pool of incredibly skilled and experienced talent.

This is a huge opportunity. I'll show you what an on-demand talent strategy looks like and how you can apply it to your company's projects.

It's Time to Get Up to SPEED

The SPEED™ strategy enables managers to build flexible, project-based teams that get results. SPEED provides an agile and flexible framework for creating on-demand teams, and it also provides the ability to adapt to unanticipated business changes. SPEED encompasses the best practices that I have observed, learned, and implemented in hundreds of projects in every type of cost, management, and operational situation. This isn't theory. These are proven steps that others have found success with, and my intention is for you to also realize success.

S-P-E-E-D stands for Success, Plan, Execute, Evaluate and Decide. Let's review each step.

S: Success

What does success look like for you?

First, begin with your project goals. If you don't know where you need to go, it's impossible to tell if you're on track to get there.

Then determine the desired outcome for the project; that will help set you on a path to achieve project success. Also consider how the project contributes to your company's goals. That way you can frame your needs for a successful project more clearly. Take time to consider the most important outcome. Also, you are much better off when you are clear about the expertise and experience that's needed.

I frequently see managers moving too rapidly to try to get everything done, without taking the time to pause and reflect on the strategies that will lead to a successful project. Review your desired project outcomes often, because external factors, company vision and direction, competition, and market forces, to name a few, can cause strategies to change and priorities to shift.

P: Plan

Once you are clear that your project's success will mean bringing in a specialist, it's time to form a plan designed to meet your goals and priorities in order to fill the talent gap you have.

The planning process starts with the drafting of a comprehensive project description. Planning then segues to the project budget, rates for the expert, ways to access the expert talent, and the screening/interviewing guidelines.

E: Execute

The key to successful execution of the project is setting and then meeting expectations. Execution comprises documenting the project deliverables in a Statement of Work (SOW), onboarding, and then integrating the consultant into your team.

The SOW defines who and what will be delivered and by when. This phase is about the nitty gritty: for example, define the invoice schedule and discuss payment terms.

Efficiently integrating the onboarded consultants with existing employees is critical so that everyone can work together in harmony. Management must clearly communicate how the consultants will help the entire team and how the project will help achieve company goals. You will need to make sure the team accepts the consultant as part of the team. Equally important is for you to ensure that the consultant can thrive in the company's culture; this is an ongoing process.

At Simplicity, we conduct a kick-off meeting at the beginning of every project where we not only discuss the work deliverables, but also the culture and the integration process for the consultant. The details of the kick-off/onboarding process are described in the next chapter.

E: Evaluate

Metrics are vital to understanding if your investment is generating the intended ROI, and they are also an early warning system for you to get ahead of possible issues. Every company has their own evaluation tools, and the most common ones that I'll share with you in the next chapter are scorecards and dashboards. These are usually basic Excel or Word documents that contain the project's key success metrics or KPIs (key performance indicators). I recommend as few KPIs as possible (I have seen scorecards with hundreds of metrics that are not useful for anyone) so that you can spot business trends quickly and adjust your strategy if needed.

Scorecards and dashboards can be calculated on a weekly or monthly basis depending on your business cycles. As business needs change, it's important to continuously evaluate the KPIs and eliminate those that are no longer meaningful—i.e., that no longer are serving the project's objectives—while adding ones that are relevant.

D: Decide

When you have achieved your project goals, you will feel empowered to tackle the next project in a faster and more efficient way. But first it's time to decide if the project remains a priority. If so, then keep going and perhaps expand it. If not, decide if it is time to shut it down.

Decisions are made with data from the evaluation step. Over time you begin to notice trends that will aid you in making informed decisions. Sometimes a program should end, and other times it should expand. Having clear metrics (see Evaluate) fosters confidence in your decisions and provides support for your manager if needed.

The SPEED strategy helps you identify what your goals are, helps you find your on-demand experts, starts the project with clear expectations, measures the results, and takes action to keep going or to pivot in another direction.

Why SPEED Works

Looks Beyond Organizational Lines

First and foremost, SPEED enables you to have a much broader viewpoint than simply placing names on an organization chart. It's about asking what your business needs and goals are and what talent and skills you'll need to achieve them.

Because businesses frequently have to do more with less, companies large and small are beginning to see the critical need for project-based, on-demand teams.

SPEED allows a company to augment its core team with on-demand talent who possess the specific skills and expertise each project needs. This keeps the core business running without distracting or overloading the FTEs with specific roles that aren't in their wheelhouse.

In addition, with veteran FTEs, there's always the danger of burnout or career plateauing. FTEs can also get stuck in the mentality of doing things "the way they've always been done." Whereas experts can produce fresh ideas and solutions, and they can inject new energy that "lifts all boats with the tide."

Focuses on Deliverables

Conventional strategy usually follows a generic, vanilla approach to talent acquisition: you have X positions available, so you fill them with X people and your job is (supposedly) done. It's a numbers game, a matter of quantity over quality, even for managers who do their best to try to find the right person for each position. When you're not clear on what you need beyond simply filling a position, your job becomes a guessing game. You choose the most qualified person you can, given your limited time, budget, and generic job descriptions, and then you cross your fingers and hope they work out.

When implementing SPEED, on the other hand, you ask one simple question: "What is the outcome needed *right now*?" The answer to this question will provide the clarity to guide your search and allow you to identify the expert with the skills you need to deliver the best outcome for your company.

For example, Michael decided the most important responsibility of the marketing manager role he was trying to fill was the ability to manage a global campaign launch. He was able to focus on prioritizing "global launch experience" as the No. 1 criteria among the available people. This clarity enabled him to quickly filter through a mountain of generic information and resumes.

Knowing Your Priorities

In general our society, and the world of managers in particular, is hectic and stressful, and there's only so much we can do to mitigate that.

When trying to do more with less, it comes down to choosing a few crucial things and doing them exceptionally well, an approach author Greg McKeown calls "essentialism."[3] As the subtitle of his book suggests, it's about the "disciplined pursuit of less." It's vital for managers to prioritize goals and answer questions such as, "What's the most important task I need someone to do for us right now?" Once you are clear on the answer, then it's a matter of making sure you have the resources to help you access the expert talent needed.

When it comes to finding the right person for the project, you're never going to get everything *and* the kitchen sink. The notion of holding out for the "perfect" candidate wastes too much time, effort, and money.

Rather than trying to "have it all," what managers should really ask is, "Of all the things the person who will fill this role will need to accomplish, what's the most important thing?" Every time I've asked a client this question, they've known immediately what that one thing is—it's amazing how quickly you can cut through the noise when you simply focus on that essential thing. Whether you need someone who has launched a global campaign or someone who has marketed to the government, simply asking this basic question makes all the difference.

Thinks Strategically

Managers often think the position they're seeking to fill is purely tactical. They incorrectly interpret strategic work as the sort that's done only by the head honchos or by expensive consultants who compose pretty PowerPoint presentations but don't do any "real" work. However, the need for strategic thinking weaves through almost every job, even those that seem largely tactical.

I've had clients assert, "I don't need anyone to do the strategy. I do the strategy. I just need someone to execute it." And that's fine; as a manager, you're completely entitled to run things that way. But execution involves strategic thinking. All roles require that each person understands how their position relates to the overall picture: someone who can problem-solve, who hears your company's needs and connects the dots. And in large, multi-level corporations, someone who knows how to work across departments, navigate red tape, and build relationships is needed. In smaller companies and start-ups, what's required is someone who's comfortable wearing different hats and taking initiative: these are strategic skills. Even if the work is tactical, a successful outcome requires thinking strategically about how to best get the work done.

I call these people the "strategic doers." Building an on-demand team of such strategic doers gives you powerful advantages in terms of greater productivity, efficiency, and cost savings.

Project-Based Environment

When thinking in terms of strategic priorities, the easiest way to break them down is by project. Some projects are big; some are small. Some are short term and more tactical; others are long term and more strategic. Each project can be broken down into even more specific tasks. A social media marketing strategy, for instance, consists of smaller sub-projects such as determining the objective for social media, determining what value your social media will provide to your audience, selecting the best channels to use and their different advantages and strategies, engaging with influencers, connecting with other communities, analyzing metrics, and developing an evolving strategy to identify and target your ideal audience.

Teams of FTEs blended with specialist consultants are better equipped to quickly deliver high-impact results for your project.

Fills the Gaps in Your Current Team

As a manager, it's essential to understand and identify the gaps in your existing team. Too many managers approach a new project's needs with the mindset of, "Well, this is the staff I have and that's just the way that it is. We've got to get all this work done, so let's just divvy it up as best we can." They don't stop to ask if they have the right team members or if they have each person doing the right things. They assume they're "stuck" with the team they have, when in reality it's within their power to create precisely the team they want.

If you identify a skills gap or feel you need additional expertise and insight to help ensure the success of the project, you can turn to an on-demand team of experts. The key is to recognize this and not try to force a task on a team member who isn't qualified or doesn't have the time for it. I often see companies shuffling people around when there's a new project to be completed, assigning tasks to those they hope can get the tasks done rather than determining if they have people with the necessary skills, or finding those that do.

As Jim Collins writes in his book *Good to Great*:

> "The executives who ignited the transformations from good to great did not first figure out where to drive the bus and then get people to take it there. No, they *first* got the right people on the bus (and the wrong people off the bus) and *then* figured out where to drive it. They

said, in essence, 'Look, I don't really know where we should take this bus. But I know this much: If we get the right people on the bus, the right people in the right seats, and the wrong people off the bus, then we'll figure out how to take it someplace great.'[4]

Once you see where the gaps are, you have the ability to get the experts on the bus who can supplement your current team on an as-needed basis. I often see consultants not only deliver on their project but add value to the existing FTE team and transfer important knowledge and skills, making the team better when they are there and when they are gone.

Sometimes gaps can occur suddenly, as in the case of a health or personal emergency. In other cases, such as parental leave, there is time to plan. In each case, however, the question becomes: who does the work?

It might be a natural reaction for managers to spread the work to existing team members. That strategy could create problems however. Some team members could naturally assume they'll be loaded up with more work temporarily because they are expected to be a "team player." It's possible the team members impacted by the increased responsibilities could resent managing the increased workload, thus negatively impacting their well-being, productivity, and dedication to the company.

Using SPEED, managers can move quickly to fill both parental and sudden leave gaps without overburdening existing employees, while keeping business goals on track.

Nimble

Using the SPEED strategy, consultants are brought in as needed—and sometimes on short notice—to work on fast-tracked projects with short deadlines. If obstacles arise, they are poised to deal with them and keep moving.

An on-demand team is "plug and play" ready, so to speak, and able to hit the ground running. Having an on-demand team also doesn't require a timely (and costly) onboarding process. It has fluidity built-in: it starts with your business priorities, which often change, so your strategy is also evolving to adapt to your latest needs.

Sometimes these needs will dictate filling your talent gaps with FTEs; sometimes you'll require one consultant; sometimes your needs will call for a group of consultants. You're free to respond to the changing needs of your business with a flexibility and quickness that conventional practices don't allow.

Leverages a Broad Network

As I noted in Chap. 1, forget about a "talent shortage." With an on-demand, project-based team, you're able to quickly access a broader group of experts than conventional talent pipelines. For example, say you need to find someone with project management skills to fill a gap in your current team. The conventional approach would be to use a recruiter (internal or external) to send candidates that meet your job description. And that's not necessarily "wrong," but you limit your options by only searching for FTEs—because it is a limited network. By leveraging a broader network, you look beyond FTEs and tap into the larger talent pool of available consultants and freelancers.

Develop trusted relationships with several agencies that have different areas of expertise you can call on. Knowing when to leverage your network of individuals and when to turn to a talent agency is part of a smart, holistic strategy.

Budget-Friendly

When you're dealing with budget cuts or a limited budget, you're forced to consider new options and new ways to get things done. Your job is easier when you have an unlimited budget, but how often does that happen? Budget cuts inspire you to get better at creative problem-solving.

Not only can on-demand teams be utilized on a tight budget, they are the best way to handle budgetary restrictions.

Leveraging experts who are highly versed in their field is not only time effective—they can get to the heart of the matter and get to it fast—but it's also cost effective. You pay only for the vital work you need done immediately, not the overhead and ongoing costs (development, training, severance, benefits) that go along with hiring FTEs. Supplementing your core of FTEs with specialists on an as-needed, per-project basis allows you more budget flexibility and control of your variable and fixed costs.

Navigating with Michael

Let's take a look at how he would approach his situation using SPEED.

Michael would step back from his overwhelming to-do list and consider which of his project goals is the top priority (SUCCESS). Let's say he determines that he could drive a significant increase in sales of a particular software product if he runs a channel incentive program with a key channel partner (PLAN). He drafts a performance-based job description and leverages the power of his network to find Amy, a highly skilled partner channel consultant with 15 years of experience under her belt (EXECUTE). Having done much of this kind of work before, Amy hits the ground running and adds immediate value, creating a program beyond Michael's initial vision that quickly increases software sales more than he had hoped for (EVALUATE). As Michael enters budget planning for the next fiscal year, he chooses to expand the channel incentive program (DECIDE) to build on its early success.

The company's sales steadily climb. The pressure eases for Michael. Michael's team can stay focused on doing their jobs while Amy spearheads the new program.

This scenario demonstrates how companies can access the experts they need to build flexible teams in concert with their FTEs to meet goals, innovate, and manage costs.

Building on-demand teams isn't a "one and done" task. There is always a need for constant refinement, re-examination, and revision to respond to a rapidly changing business landscape.

In Chap. 4 I'll take you through the SPEED strategy and teach you how to successfully build on-demand teams.

Notes

1. Based on a response to a November 2015 email survey.
2. Scott Brinker and Laura McLellan, "The Rise of the Chief Marketing Technologist," *Harvard Business Review,* July–August 2014. Available at https://hbr.org/2014/07/the-rise-of-the-chief-marketing-technologist
3. Greg McKeown, *Essentialism: The Disciplined Pursuit of Less* (New York: Crown Publishing Group, 2014).
4. Jim Collins, *Good to Great: Why Some Companies Make the Leap…And Others Don't* (New York: HarperCollins Publishers Inc., 2001), p. 41.

CHAPTER 4

Build Your On-Demand Team

I look at my talent pool holistically. I sometimes hire consultants if I think a project will be short-term, rather than hire a full time employee, but once I've looked at my needs I don't assume what kind of role each position will be. I spend time evaluating the role and the type of employee that best suits it at that particular time. I look at my staffing needs and then I choose between multiple options and resources to set up the staff.

—Amanda F., technology company manager

I introduced SPEED™ in the previous chapter, and here I'll take you through the SPEED strategy in detail, with questions for reflection at the end of each section. Whether you choose to bring in specialists on your own or hire a company that places talent, you will learn how to access specialized talent for project-based work in a fast, flexible way.

Regardless of your company's size or whether it has a formalized supplier process for accessing talent, elements of SPEED can be integrated into your own business. (Note that the

SPEED strategy does not apply to accessing FTEs.) SPEED encompasses the best practices that I have learned while working on thousands of projects. SPEED isn't a theory. What I will share is a practical and easy process for you to integrate into your business and by doing so, achieve the success I have seen many managers experience.

S: Success

Take time to identify the most important outcome. How will you know when you achieve project success? How does the project contribute to the company goals? The answers to these questions will help you frame your needs for a successful project more clearly. Also, you are much better off when you are clear about what expertise and experience you need.

You have many talent needs and goals, but if you focus on one major project outcome you'd like to achieve, you gain the clarity that will help you fast-track the process. Then, determine the result you want to see in 30-60-90 days. You may have an epiphany, as many of my clients have had once they have a good idea of what success looks like. Next, look at your team and evaluate their expertise to see if there is a talent gap that needs to be filled to implement and complete the project successfully. In many cases, I have seen managers who realize they have a talent gap, but that realization didn't happen until they took the time to evaluate and define the requirements for their project's success. Also make sure the successful outcome of the project coincides with and contributes to your company's larger goals.

Revisit your definition of success frequently and carve out time to think about what is essential to achieve success.

Roberta, a manager at a wireless company, told me how she defined success.

> "When I started looking at the programs and projects on my plate that would directly impact our company goals, I realized I had some skill gaps. Looking at my staffing requirements, I asked myself: Am I going to just hire FTEs? Am I going to have enough budget if I need a specialist on the project, whether it's a consultant or a contractor or an intern? What is my mix going to look like?"

A good analogy for defining success is to consider how you choose a doctor. You wouldn't go to a general practitioner for heart surgery—you would choose a heart surgeon. The same goes for the makeup of your team. If you want a digital marketing expert, you don't hire a marketing manager with little digital experience. You are choosing to hire specialists, not generalists; that is one of the huge advantages of building on-demand teams. When hiring consultants, you don't have to go through the expense and time it takes to hire and train a full-time employee. Identifying your organization's priorities and the specialists needed for the project is where to focus your time.

Once you have taken the time to know what your priorities for success are, it's easier to identify existing skill gaps. Evaluate your current team members: draw a chart with boxes that lists skills—rather than names. Then look at your current team and identify who has the right expertise. This is an important step, because it's natural for most organizations to first start with the names of the people and move them around. However, optimizing for the expertise and skills needed for a project's goals—without emphasis on names and titles—will help you achieve your objectives faster.

Look beyond the name and title of each person already in your organization to assess and determine whether their strengths and skills match the expertise needed for the project.

Let's say that increasing your company's brand awareness is a priority. You draw your team organization chart and realize that you don't have anyone with PR expertise, or perhaps PR has been someone's side job or was relegated to an intern or junior employee. The public relations industry has radically changed over the last few years. You need a team member knowledgeable in those changes and the new tools and platforms available.

Questions for Reflection

- How do you define a successful project?
- What is the most important business goal that you can contribute to your organization?
- What up-to-date, relevant expertise do you need to accomplish your goals?
- What are the skill gaps on your team?

P: Planning

When it is clear that you don't have the in-house expertise necessary for your project, it's time to form a plan designed to meet your goals and priorities in order to fill a talent gap.

Project Description

At this point, you'll craft a project description that specifies what the consultant will do. It's essential to do this before you talk to candidates. Because you want the expert to hit the ground running and add immediate value to the project, clearly specify their role, skills, and responsibilities.

I have worked with managers who were searching for certain types of expertise that they either didn't understand or weren't up to date in. This situation made it difficult to craft the specifics of the project description. If you find yourself in this situation, you can turn to a trusted peer in the industry who is an expert for insight. Also, if you are working with an agency that has expertise in placing specialized talent, they can often be invaluable in helping you draft a comprehensive and accurate project description.

The project description is your best marketing vehicle for your company, so make sure you write a compelling description. The more clarity the better: with an accurate project description, you'll attract and match the candidate(s) with the right skills and experience.

The project description should include the following elements:

Base Your Description on Performance: Orient the project description to performance rather than a list of duties. Make it "do" oriented versus "have" oriented. For example, instead of saying, "We need a seasoned project manager with five years of relevant experience," say instead, "We need a project manager who has led multiple, global-scale projects managing 20-plus work streams and has delivered projects on time and on budget." Frame everything from the perspective of what you want and expect. What do I want this person to do? What will they deliver? What result will I see in 30-60-90 days?

Emphasize Your Company's Value: Craft the description to attract high performers who will deliver results every time. The sought-after specialists/consultants select projects with companies that inspire them—they want to make an impact and be part of something exciting. If you want to attract them, don't use your company's boilerplate "About Us" in the project description. Sell the specialists on the opportunity to deliver high-impact work on a project that will transform the organization, and be an integral part of something that matters while adding value to the company.

Also, make sure the project description includes your company's strengths. For example, "We are a fast-growing tech company changing the online payment processing industry and looking for high-impact digital marketing consultants to help lead our growth." This is more engaging than, "We are an online payment processing company in need of digital marketing consultants." See the difference?

The description should stress the importance of the project and the value it brings to the company. For many candidates, the attraction is the project itself, not necessarily the money. "I look for projects where I can really dig in, solve problems and make a difference. If I hear about a role and get excited, then that is the right role for me. I like projects where I can come in and be a strategic doer—I create the strategy and then execute against it, allowing the client to focus on other areas of their job," said Hannah M., a project consultant.

For Fred Talmadge, a freelance software and app developer based in Seattle, it's about learning. He has experienced profound changes in his life since he started freelancing in 2011. "Professionally, I learn more every day by working on different types of projects of my choosing as a freelancer, and it keeps things fresh," he said.[1]

Clarity about your project will attract the right candidates, and that will help you when you get to the screening and interviewing phase to sort through all the candidates.

Other factors to include in the project description are whether you are implementing a strategic or tactical role. Do you need a strategist, a tactician, or a combination?

Clarify Whether You Need On-Site Talent: Do they have to be on site? Or, will they be on site only on certain days or for meetings? How close to your company's location should they be? The answer for any project is that it depends. Some companies like to see the consultant regularly, but that can change once the project is underway. The location, schedule, and hours depend on the level of trust you have with the person.

For example, a financial analyst consultant who worked for a large software company in Washington moved her family to Texas, but because her expertise was so valued, the company hired her on a project basis to help them with various ad hoc projects. She had earned the team's trust to do the work anywhere. The company retained her valuable knowledge, and the consultant could work on a schedule that made sense for her situation and time zone.

Clarify Expectations for Schedule/Hours: Another consideration is whether your talent should be part time or full time. When FTEs are overloaded with their work deliverables and administration duties, it can be hard to show progress in key areas. Sometimes a part-time expert is all you need—this can be a low-cost way to drive big impact for your business. I often meet clients who need specific expertise on a 10- or 20-hour per week basis. By having the client identify the key priority and then hiring an expert to do only that on a part-time contract, the company is able to achieve its goal within budget. This is often the smartest solution; sometimes a part-time expert is all you will need to drive the project.

A well-crafted project description provides a tight focus during the screening process—so that you know the skills you are seeking and what questions to ask.

Plan Budgets and Rates

Don't waste precious time interviewing candidates until you know your budget. Budgets play a key role in determining schedules and hours. To hire an expert on a project basis, managers will usually have to tap into their marketing dollars or discretionary budgets. Confirm the funding is there before you begin talking to candidates. Otherwise it's embarrassing and a waste of time if you identify a great candidate, draft the SOW, and are ready to begin the project—and then realize the funds are not there. It's an obvious point, but I have seen this happen.

Fair rates for the consultant(s) can fluctuate depending on the market and the skills required for the project. Budgets, the industry market, and rates are more art than science. The factors to weigh are:

- How much budget is available?
- How much demand is there for the expertise needed?
- How much demand is there for the specific consultant(s) you are interested in?

Get a sense of the range of market value by asking your colleagues what they are paying for similar expertise and by searching sites like payscale.com and salary.com for the pay ranges in your particular region for the expertise you need. You should also consider the fully-burdened (total) cost of an employee you would hire. If you hired an FTE for that same role, you would add at least 25–50% to their salary to account for employer taxes, state and federal taxes, benefits, stock, office space and overhead costs, and more.

Let's say you want to hire a project manager on a contract and you want to pay a fair market rate to attract the best talent, but you also have a lot of other important projects that you need to reserve your budget for. You determine, based on asking your colleagues and doing some research on the web, that if you hired this role as a FTE it would be in the range of a fully-burdened cost of $250,000 annually. Then, you find a project manager expert whose bill rate is $125–150/hour depending on the scope of the work. Doing the math, you determine that this rate seems fair because it's in the market value range. Annualizing the consultant's pay would come to about $250,000–$300,000 per year, but it's important to note that most consultants do not work full-time all year, and you might not need them for a full year.[2]

One shift I have noticed is that some clients are moving away from agencies with annual retainers in the millions of dollars, and instead are bringing in individual experts who are more nimble – at a fraction of the price. I worked with a large online company that saved thousands of dollars each month by replacing an outside agency with in-house consultants to work on the project. Not only did the company save money, it was able to get things done much faster with a smaller, agile team. For some large-scale projects, using a large agency might be needed. But I've observed a growing trend where companies tap on-demand experts to work directly with them. Budgets can go further using individual consultants or a team of consultants as opposed to paying for the hierarchy and overhead included in a large agency's retainer.

Accessing Talent

For on-demand projects, it can be difficult to access experts using the conventional sources for finding FTEs. Professionals who work on projects can be found through multiple channels depending on whether managers are looking to find talent on their own, typically within small and midsize companies, or whether the manager must work within the constraints of formalized supplier guidelines for large corporations. There is no one-size-fits-all approach because every company is unique, but there are some common channels available to access consultants.

The overview below shows a progression of options and sources for finding experts on-demand that you can do by yourself or by working with an agency. You probably are aware of most of these, but you'll need to use them with a new focus and advanced filters for finding the right expert(s) for your project.

- **Word-of-Mouth Referrals:** The old adage that it is all about your Rolodex rings true—even if you don't know what a Rolodex is. Word of mouth, or WOM, is the most common avenue to tap experts when you need them. It's the "know, like, trust" concept—we trust what our peers think, and their recommendations hold extra weight with us because we know them and we believe they have our best interests in mind. Ask who they have worked with in this role. Even if someone in your immediate network doesn't know anyone with the special expertise you are seeking, they most likely know someone who does. Each search should expand your network for the next time you need a consultant. There are great programs, such as Evernote and OneNote, to keep your list of expanding names, organized by expertise, within reach at any time. If someone is referred to you, make sure to review their past performance. Just because they are recommended doesn't mean you should overlook validating their work and past performance.

- **Job Posting/Search Sites:** Job posting sites have become very common for companies to post jobs and for people looking for work to search for jobs and/or post their resume. Finding consultants can be more difficult on these sites. It takes some digging to find the diamonds in the rough on these platforms, and just because you can reach a lot of people easily doesn't mean that quantity will equal quality. Again, having a well-defined and targeted project description to attract the best candidates enables you to better filter the information on job boards, if you choose to use them.

- **LinkedIn:** LinkedIn is by no means inclusive or representative of all the talent that's out there, but it can be of value in finding consultants for your project. You can search for talent using its "Advanced Search" feature: In the keyword field, you can type in "consultant" or even more specifically, "digital marketing consultant." You will quickly view anyone in your network with that title. This approach only taps your network, so it is limited. You can also spend a lot of time going through this process, weeding through people who aren't the right fit in the hope you'll be lucky enough to land on one or two who are. It's extremely similar to culling through resumes, only on a large scale and with the difference being that using LinkedIn to find consultants requires an additional step: you will need to determine their availability, as the platform doesn't offer that feature. LinkedIn can also function as a job board for posting your project description. (Note: There are plenty of talented experts who aren't on LinkedIn or, if they are, they're not necessarily looking at job posts or thinking about promoting themselves on that platform, so their profiles aren't optimized in a way that will make them show up in your searches).

- **Freelance Marketplaces and Platforms:** This is an emerging sector that covers general business marketplaces of talent as well as specialized industry-specific platforms, such as engineering, private equity, HR, finance, marketing, and more. These platforms connect businesses with freelancers worldwide and offer an efficient way to post projects and search for exactly the skills you need for a project. Your detailed project description can be posted on these platforms, and each has different tools that enable you to check specific freelancers' credibility, endorsements, and portfolios of work. The most important thing to look for in these platforms is the credibility of the talent that they promote. Some are simply matchmaking services, and they don't take any responsibility for screening, interviewing, or placement. Others provide more "full-service" offerings, including extensive profiles, background checks, and more. Their fee structures vary. Depending on your needs, evaluating the suitability of some of these platforms could widen your talent pool. In the Resource Guide, we have listed some of 2015s top sites for finding freelance talent.

• **Specialized Agencies:** Another strong and growing option is to leverage the knowledge and access of an agency to find the best consultant(s) for your project. The benefit of working with an agency is that it's faster than finding consultants on your own. Specialized agencies are part of a competitive and growing field. Large consulting companies "will face fierce competition" from the smaller, specialized agencies, according to a 2015 trend report from Plunkett Research. "In particular, consultancies that can quickly improve their clients' profits may have the best competitive advantage over the mid-term," the report continued. Further, corporate clients may lean toward hiring consultancies that have a proven ability "not only to point out a corporation's problems and strategic deficiencies, but also to implement solutions that cut debt, restore health to balance sheets and stabilize profits."[3] I talk to companies every day that want what I call a "strategic doer," someone to cut through the bureaucracy and quickly get the work done. Working with the right agency that can bring you the specialized industry experts you need is often the best, most cost-effective, and fastest solution. Whatever industry you need an expert in—HR, marketing and sales, finance, etc.—there are talent placement companies that focus on that particular industry. They have expert talent that thoroughly understands their specific industries. Working with an agency can help you achieve your project goals faster and grow your business in a couple of months rather than a year or longer. You should expect the agency to know your business and your culture. A goal should be for your agency to become a trusted partner, an asset to your company, and your go-to resource. The acumen and talent on tap that the agency brings to your company afford you the ability to have the right talent with the up-to-date industry skills you need. In the Resource Guide, we list some of the elements that go into evaluating a talent agency.

- **Approved Supplier List:** If you work for a large company you might have an approved supplier list for accessing talent. Leverage your internal resources to help you identify the right talent for your project needs. Ask your colleagues for the references of the suppliers they've worked with who have done similar work. You can learn a lot about an existing supplier's reputation and quality of work if the supplier has had a long-standing relationship and a verifiable track record of success with your company. You may also find that you have to go through your company's internal process to get a new supplier approved if you can't find the talent or industry-specific expertise you need on the approved list.

Screening

SPEED enables fast and agile decision making during the screening and interviewing process.

Once you have a list of potential candidates, whether you have obtained them from your network referrals or from your company's formal supplier program, time is of the essence. You must have a system where you can quickly make educated and sound judgments about people's ability. The most important thing to remember is that past performance will likely predict future performance, so get to the heart of the person's work background quickly.

Typically consultants have worked on a wide range of projects, so you'll have a history of their success to review. Their experience at a wide range of companies and with many projects will be an asset to you and your project. Consultants with an extensive project history in their portfolios provide a roadmap of their experiences and successes for managers to evaluate. This counters the old-fashioned perception that a long period of uninterrupted work on a resume is the most stable and desirable asset or that a candidate is "flaky" because of a work record with multiple short-term jobs listed. That perception still persists but is no longer relevant as you navigate the talent shift underway.

"He's an independent communications consultant." That's what Annie says to her dad, played by Steve Martin in the 1991 movie *Father of the Bride*, when asked what her newly engaged beau, Bryan, does for a living.

"That is code for unemployed! Perfect," a stunned Dad says. "You meet an unemployed amazingly brilliant non-ape who

I am going to have to support. I suppose I'm going to have to hire him [at my successful athletic shoe company] and fire some hard-working guy with three kids because my son-in-law, the 'independent communications consultant' can't get a job anywhere else. No wonder he will move anywhere you get a job!"[4]

The father's belief that a "consultant" means "unemployed" misrepresents the modern consultant. A great consultant can have long list of projects with short-term duration. In addition, consultants have personal brands, project/work portfolios, and often their own websites. These are different dynamics for the manager to consider during the screening process.

Seasoned consultants are experts in their industry, so as you screen them, determine how they'll use their myriad of project experience and takeaways to add value to your project.

If you are not working with an agency, but have posted the position on your own or reached out to a potential candidate recommended by your network, the screening process will need to include a determination of availability. Whether it is by email or phone, the initial contact will set the stage for the rest of the screening process. You might have a good idea that the person(s) is suitable based on your search to this point, but the first interaction will move the process forward to the interview phase.

If an agency has provided you with a list of potential candidates, I recommend a phone call before an interview. A word of caution at this stage: be aware of your biases and avoid snap judgments.

Blink by Malcolm Gladwell talks about how we make snap judgments based on our life experiences about people. He says, "The answer is that we are not helpless in the face of our first impressions. They may bubble up from the unconscious—from behind a locked door inside of our brain—but just because something is outside of awareness doesn't mean it's outside of control."[5]

Interviewing

Most managers are adept at hiring FTEs already, but there are both similarities and differences when hiring an expert. The similarities are that first impressions are as powerful when hiring an expert as when hiring an FTE, but those things aren't as relevant as the work they have done and what they can do for you.

Another similarity is that you should keep the interview focused on what you need and how the candidate's past performance is applicable. By taking this approach, you will know within the first 10 minutes if you have a good fit.

We are naturally attracted to people like ourselves; it makes us feel safe. But the value in being open to different thoughts, approaches, and people is that we gain a diverse perspective and background. Diversity is a secret sauce that can foster innovation and help grow your company. It starts with the manager, who is after all an FTE, recognizing his or her preferences and attitudes and putting them aside to focus on the need for a different way of doing things through a consultant.

Here are some differences when hiring a consultant:

In the interview, instead of starting with a generic "tell me about yourself" statement and letting the candidate take that conversation anywhere they want, ask them about their specific project contributions and accomplishments. The best candidates are comfortable with sharing their past successes and can relate what they have accomplished in previous projects to your needs.

For example, ask about their most important contribution; they should articulate the value they delivered for a previous client and show that with a presentation of their work results. If you interview a consultant who appears unprepared and answers questions generically, such as, "I worked on a large team and we all had different roles and, ultimately, the project was a great success," that's not enough information: it doesn't tell the manager anything about the candidate's specific contribution. It raises questions because they are not saying anything concrete about their work.

Here's a great example of a consultant who came prepared and added value during the interview process. I was working with a large software company that needed a retail merchandising expert to help increase its in-store phone sales. The consultant went to the retailer where the phone was sold and observed the marketing and sales associate's knowledge of the product. Based on her expertise, she drafted a high-level plan of what she would do differently to increase sales. She shared her ideas during the interview and immediately began brainstorming with the company on ways to increase sales.

This made an impression because the candidate immediately demonstrated the value she could deliver. A manager could immediately see how the person works, thinks, and problem-solves, thus increasing your confidence.

Great consultants don't necessarily want to spend a lot of time talking about theory or generalities, they would rather roll up their sleeves and get into the mix to help you address your project needs and challenges now. That's what you want to see: candidates that demonstrate how they can add value to the project and are excited to get started.

Success in bringing in a consultant hinges largely on determining what they know about—and how they might fit into—the company's culture, along with their soft skills. Hard skills are easy to identify and are part of the consultant's resume, as well as their experience, accreditations, and qualifications. If the manager looks only at hard skills, it's difficult to determine if there is a good fit because they are looking only at one dimension when they really want to look at every dimension, including the "nuances" of team dynamics and company culture.

Managers don't get that full picture until the actual interview process. Treat the interview as a sort of dry run for how the candidate might approach the project. Why not invite them to work with the project team for a day?

For instance, have the consultant(s) come in and give them a problem to solve. Put the problem on a whiteboard and observe how they respond. Don't expect a perfect answer, because they don't know your business yet, but it's a great way to see how they think on their feet. If you like the way they think and/or how they problem-solve as well as the questions that they fire back at you, then put them on a 30-day, or even a three-month, contract and get them started doing the work.

Remember, you are not hiring a FTE; don't spend a huge amount of time combing through resumes. A short-term contract can have very clear metrics associated with the role, and if the consultant is not meeting your expectations, have a conversation, determine why it is not working and what should happen to make it work.

Cultural Fit

Another important aspect of the interview is a determination of whether a cultural fit is there. You have to be clear about your company's culture and who would work well with your team on the project. Is your company community driven? Or, does it have an entrepreneurial spirit? What types of personalities would do well in your shop? Cultural fit works both ways—for yourself and the candidate. Ask if the candidate has previously worked in entrepreneurial environments, and how that worked out. Find out how he or she has performed in a similar culture. Have the candidate give examples of how they have done this job before, either as an FTE or as a contractor, and how they would accomplish the goals in your company's culture.

Also ask how they deal with ambiguity. For example, the candidate might relate that he or she had to hit a certain metric on a project with very little direction—and here's how the situation was handled. This type of interaction gets into real-world scenarios and shows how the candidate performed in that kind of environment.

Great consultants consistently bring a high energy level to their work and are excited to work on a product or service they love. As you interview, observe their energy, conviction, and acumen.

Here are a few questions to focus on when interviewing:

1. Tell me about your last project; what was your contribution to its success?

   Tip: Follow up by asking the candidate to list the project's team on a whiteboard or piece of paper, with a description of their role, who their managers/clients were, and their colleagues. You are looking for past performance: their contributions and consistency. This gives you more information about their role on a team, their collaboration style, and possible references in addition to those you previously gathered from the candidate. It's a good idea to request three examples that illustrate consistency and expertise on the project.

2. Tell me about a time when you failed on a project; what did you learn from that experience?

   Tip: You are looking for resilience, adaptability, and self-awareness. It may be hard to determine, but you are looking for consultants who see growth as part of their professional life. Are they continuing to seek out new certifications, training, and knowledge within their industry?

3. What would your most recent manager/client say that your three key strengths are?

Tip: You are looking for awareness about how others view their strengths and skills and how they work with others. Watch how they respond. If they are evasive or fidgety or talk about how the previous team was difficult to work with, those could be red flags that the candidate has trouble working with others. Also, it might be a sign they are not a team player.

ABCs

When searching, screening, and interviewing for a great consultant, I recommend looking for the ABCs: a great attitude, the ability to gain and build trust, and effective communication skills. When I first started my company, I asked my clients what they looked for in a great consultant, and time and again I heard them say that they wanted someone with a go-getter Attitude who could Build trust and be a great Communicator. These skills appear obvious, yet these seemingly small things are the important attributes and differentiators between what makes a good and a great consultant. I have placed thousands of consultants over the years and found that the ABCs are the attributes of the great ones.

Great Attitude The best consultants are proven, high-energy performers who inject enthusiasm and excitement into their projects. They gain satisfaction by helping their clients be successful and have a contagious energy and aura that attracts clients, and as a result, they are frequently approached by companies about more work.

Build Trust The best consultants know how to build trust, and they are a trusted partner to their clients. They think ahead; after meetings, they follow up with notes and plan for key events before their client does. They take care of the details and consistently show up for the client. They do what they say they will do.

Clear Communication Being able to communicate well in PowerPoint, in email, and verbally are non-negotiable skills. Clear, concise communication is a must have. I have had several clients tell me that if they receive a long-winded email from a consultant that has no point, they delete it and question the consultant's credibility.

Questions for Reflection

- Do you have the appropriate budget approval to bring on a consultant?
- Have you written a compelling project description that you have shared broadly?
- Do you have a good understanding of the hard skills, soft skills, and cultural fit needed.
- Have you gathered the consultant's performance data from the interview process?

E: Execute

Once you have your consultant(s) on board, the key to successful execution of the project is setting and then meeting expectations. After all, setting the project up for success is in everyone's best interest. Execution comprises documenting project deliverables in a Statement of Work (SOW), onboarding, and integrating your consultant into your team.

Statement of Work (SOW)

A SOW is a high-level document that describes the work to be done, the timeline, and the invoicing schedule. Writing everything down is essential to setting the project up for success. Do not move forward with only a handshake. It's very common for needs to shift and your deliverables to need adjustment, so you want the SOW to be a living document that you refer to often to stay on track. The more detailed the document, the better. As business changes occur, discuss them with the consultant and them in. Keeping the SOW up to date minimizes possible misunderstandings on priorities and the deliverables.

Onboarding and Integration

A project kick-off meeting is one of the most valuable steps in the SPEED process. The purpose of this meeting is to establish a shared and trusted working relationship between you and the consultant from day one. I have had clients tell me that they don't think the kick-off meeting is necessary—until they actually participate in one. Although your SOW is written, a 15-minute kick-off meeting sets the stage for the details of who the consultant(s) will work with, where to access documents, and other housekeeping items. The meeting will also identify metrics and communicate clear expectations to ensure success—in terms of project-tracking and reviews during the first 30 days.

The first 30 days are critical, so communication at this point about goals, culture, and logistics is better than addressing it later. Practices that are unique to a particular workplace can become big issues if they are not communicated clearly early on; minor things can become major issues, and discussing them in a kick-off meeting can be liberating. After conducting kick-off meetings for many years, I know that they improve client and consultant satisfaction, and increase productivity.

Preventing Resentment

It's crucial for full-time employees to see contractors not as "outsiders" or people taking over their jobs. Make sure your full-time employees understand that the work roles of the expert, or a team of experts, are necessary for the success of the project, and perhaps the future of the company.

Building strong blended teams of FTEs and experts with top to bottom buy-in is a critical component of the integration process. Strong communication and transparency will help the new team get off to a smooth start and prevent friction or resentment from developing early on within the team, before it can become a stumbling block. In the case of company Green, a major corporation, (see Chap. 8), "We did have weekly calls," said Diana, who managed a large transformation project for the company. "We had weekly team meetings. At one point probably for several months, we had daily rah-rahs at 7 a.m. every morning. We would have 30 people in a room and we'd say, okay, this is what we're doing. This is the focus. Here's the countdown to the next big point."

Sometimes the transition to a blended team is difficult. "There was definitely conflict," Diana noted. "It was tough. I ended up losing some people to other departments because it was an environment that was very difficult and it was very high pressure. But ultimately, most of the team realized that we needed the help so desperately that they really just wanted to sit down and be able to transfer as much knowledge and information as they could so that these experts could be super productive."

It was critical for Green employees to be committed and involved because "they knew the system, they knew the products, they knew the culture, and they knew the business," Diana continued. "They were able to work with the (consultants) to get the job done."

Mindset is important when it comes to putting together an effective team. Yes, skill sets matter, but for many projects, large and small, you also need people who are willing to adapt, be flexible, and let everyone do their own jobs to the best of their ability. Sometimes, this means accepting that the people you've brought in are there because they can do things your existing team cannot. There's no room for ego, competition, or power struggles; everyone should operate as a team and work toward the same goal rather than worrying about their individual reputations.

Because the first few weeks are critical to setting everyone up for success, here's an onboarding, best-practice plan to use during the first weeks of the consultant's participation in the project. By taking the time to do this, you will minimize future headaches and misunderstandings and see the business results you want, faster.

Week 1: Official Onboarding
As the manager, you should expect your consultant to immediately begin work on the project while helping to move it forward and/or resolve issues. Here are a few things that will aid in a more productive first week as well as during the first 30 days of the contract:

- Access to people and resources, for the consultant:
    - Badge and PC set up, if needed
    - List of aliases the consultant will need to use
    - List of relevant websites/tools
    - Introduction email to the broader team so that everyone knows who the consultant is and what the consultant is there to do

- Getting started questions to discuss together:
    - Kick-off meeting agenda
    - Definition of success

- What will success look like?
- Are there clearly defined metrics that we can measure performance against?
- How do these metrics align with client and/or team accountabilities?
- What are some of the upcoming deliverables and milestones in the SOW that must be met?
- Are there challenges the consultant will face in this role and/or in achieving goals, and what is the best approach to overcoming them?

- Points of integration:

  - Who are the key players the consultant will interact with? What does the consultant need to know about the individuals on the team?
  - What resources can the consultant access and review? (These include documents, web content, online shared plans, and more.)
  - Is there a particular process you'd like the consultant to follow if he or she is managing the project?

- Rhythm of communication:

  - What is your preferred communication style and method (direct/open, formal/informal, IM, text, etc.)?
  - Do you have a weekly status report template or would you prefer the consultant to provide it? Do you have a preference for how it is submitted?

- When do you want to schedule a recurring one-on-one meeting?

- Housekeeping:
  - What is the preferred schedule for the consultant to work on site or remotely?
  - Review the invoicing/billing schedule.
  - Confirm the consultant's work schedule, including the potential dates the consultant won't be available.

Week 2: Engagement and Access

Now that everyone understands what they are here to accomplish, make sure the consultant has what is needed to engage and access the right people and information.

Examples:

- Establish clear rules of engagement:
  - Weekly one-on-one meetings are on everyone's respective calendar.
  - Weekly status report is agreed upon (from template to delivery method).
  - List of key stakeholders is included in communications on project deliverables.
  - Confirm that all network, tools and portal permissions are granted for complete accessibility.
  - Confirm that the consultant is invited to all the key meetings and included on all of the appropriate distribution lists.

Week 3: Fine-Tuning

Now that the consultant is more knowledgeable about the details of the project, this is a good time to talk about the opportunities and/or obstacles pertaining to the deliverables of the project:

- Consultant to discuss current status of the project/ deliverables:

  - Are we running up against any obstacles? If so, what are some proposed solutions for overcoming them?
  - Are there other opportunities for the consultant to achieve the intended results and move the needle on the project?
  - Are there other team members that we need to bring into the discussion?

- Manager to discuss current status of the project/ deliverables:

  - How's the consultant's performance to date?
  - What do you want to see more of? Less of?
  - Have there been new developments that require a shift in how the consultant is prioritizing the work?

Week 4: Progress to Date

By Week 4, the manager and the consultant should be working in unison. If not, reevaluate the priorities. Get ahead of the small issues that could become major issues as soon as possible.

Here are some common issues and how to address them:

- Other team members begin asking the consultant to do work for them.

  - As part of your weekly one-on-one check-in meeting, ensure the consultant is not distracted by non-impactful work assigned from the larger team. Also, you don't want to burn out your consultant and/or pay for work not included in the SOW.

- You don't see the consultant on IM and question if they are working.

  - If your team uses IM to stay in touch and you were clear that being online during work hours was required, but you only see the consultant online sporadically during business hours, you might question whether the work is getting done. I once had a client tell me they didn't see their consultant on IM all day and wondered if they were working. I asked if the work deliverables were being met on time; she reviewed the consultant's recent deliverables and said, "No." In this case, the lack of IM use indicated that the work was not getting done.

- You hear that the consultant is not contributing in meetings.

  - Approach the consultant, share this feedback, and review with him or her the expectations of the consultant's role. Some managers do not want a consultant giving their opinion in a meeting, and other managers expect them to speak up. Make sure the consultant understands how you expect them to participate during meetings.

- Your consultant takes a day off. Should you pay for it?

  - It depends on the SOW. If your SOW is based on a list of specific deliverables, meaning you are paying a flat fee over the contract period, then do not alter that agreement, assuming the work is being done on time. If the contract is hourly, then usually the consultant will not report the hours that are not worked.

A list of onboarding issues can become lengthy, so make sure you include the items that are the most relevant for your organization—the more detail from the start the better. You'll empower the consultant to hit the ground running and deliver results faster by also using this time to share your culture's insight. Understanding "office politics," especially in large organizations, is a key to success for many people. The best and most agile consultants are adept at navigating the potential minefields; they thrive on leaving the company better off than when they arrived.

Onboarding consultants with your existing employees smoothly is critical in order for everyone to work together in harmony. This includes integrating consultants into the corporate culture quickly. Build trust with your existing team by communicating why you are bringing in a consultant i.e., they add expertise and value to achieve company and team goals. If the individuals on the team can't accept this new member, you probably won't see the results you are seeking.

Questions for Reflection

- Do I have a detailed SOW drafted that specifies all deliverables, who does what, and the timeline and payment terms?
- Have I communicated to my team the reason I am bringing in an expert and established an environment of inclusion and trust? Have I established lines of communication between the consultant and the rest of the team?
- Have I set expectations appropriately with the consultant about our culture and the work?

E: Evaluate

Once you have a consultant on board, the evaluation process begins. This is a critical phase to make sure the work is getting done as you agreed upon under the SOW and also to evaluate whether the metrics should change. It's common to start off a project with clear metrics, but things might begin to change/evolve over time. Constant evaluation of metrics is critical to making sure the goals are being met.

Scorecards and dashboards are terms used interchangeably to describe a visual, interactive way to measure progress on a particular goal or metric. You can find examples of scorecards and dashboards on the Internet; there is no perfect template, but these examples share some common components for tracking performance. These metrics can become the outcomes of your SOW; you can even track them in a simple spreadsheet with red, yellow, and green for progress to the goal each week. You can ask your consultant to manage the scorecard/dashboard. I have observed that fewer metrics are more impactful than many, but this also depends on the project. If you have 100 metrics, it's difficult, if not impossible, to spot the trends; it also takes a team of people to update the scorecard/dashboard. Determine what data is critical to track on a weekly basis. Keep the weekly scorecard/dashboard focused on the key indicators affecting the project. You will also see monthly and quarterly trends in your business reviews.

Here's an example of how a high-impact metric can spotlight a trend. Joan is managing a sales channel, and one of the key metrics is tracking spend per channel partner. She reviews this metric weekly and notices that the team is spending their budget faster than planned. So Joan investigates. One explanation could be that the channel partners are successfully selling your product; another reason might be that budget funds are being mismanaged. Either way, there's a red flag. Joan may learn that she should increase the investment to keep the channel sales positive. Or she may discover that the money *is* being mismanaged and redirects the remaining funds to other programs. By tracking a simple metric and reviewing it weekly, Joan was able to evaluate the program quickly and take the necessary action.

Questions for Reflection

- How do you evaluate success?
- What are your key metrics?

- In what format do you want to review these metrics?
- How often will you review the scorecard/dashboard?

D: Decide

When you have realized success by achieving your project goals, you feel empowered to tackle the next project in a faster and more efficient way. But first, it's time to decide if the project remains a priority. If so, then keep it going. Or maybe you should expand it, or shut it down.

Here are some considerations to include in the decision-making process:

- Review the metrics and the trends. Are you achieving your intended metrics? Do your metrics need to be modified? Was the original goal too aggressive or not aggressive enough?
- Evaluate your goals to determine if the goals are still the priority.
- Decide on alternatives: are there other paths to pursue that can achieve the business goal?

These informed decisions are important, so take time to reflect on the next course of action. Beware of "analysis paralysis." You will never have *all* the data. Making decisions is arguably the most challenging and exhausting part of a manager's job, but SPEED enables you to move your decision making forward by focusing on results.

Questions for Reflection

- Are the goals still relevant?
- Am I missing the right expertise on my team?

- Are the metrics meaningful and helping me make sound business decisions?

You now have the tools and knowledge to build an on-demand team, but you may face some obstacles along the way. Chapter 5 discusses some common roadblocks and how to overcome them.

Notes

1. Quoted in "Freelancing in America: 2015," Press release, October 1, 2015, by the Freelancers Union and Upwork. Retrieved from https://www.upwork.com/press/2015/10/01/freelancers-union-and-upwork-release-new-study-revealing-insights-into-the-almost-54-million-people-freelancing-in-america/
2. Estimated bill rates.
3. Consulting Business Trends Analysis, *Plunkett Research, Ltd.*, November 11, 2014. Retrieved from http://www.plunkettresearch.com/trends-analysis/consulting-management-business-market/
4. *Father of the Bride* dialogue from the 1991 movie. YouTube clip retrieved from https://www.youtube.com/watch?v=PBjCLFjQDkY
5. Malcolm Gladwell, *Blink: The Power of Thinking Without Thinking* (New York: Little, Brown and Company, 2005).

CHAPTER 5

Overcoming Roadblocks and Perceptions

*T*here are some people who like to cause change because change is what's needed. They want to move on to something that's broken and fix it.

—*Richard T, software executive*

I've said that how you start is how you finish, and the biggest factor many decision makers will face is shifting their—and their company's—mindsets and perceptions about the use of on-demand, expert talent for strategic projects.

Once you've adopted the SPEED™ strategy and understand how to work effectively with consultants to achieve your team's project goals, you might take on another role, as Michael did. Do you remember Michael from Chap. 3? His budget was cut and he urgently needed expert help on a project. You probably have guessed that Michael adopted SPEED. But first he had to shift his mindset from a conventional FTE "hiring" approach in order to embrace the SPEED strategy. Once he saw there was a different way to think about and acquire talent, it was a major breakthrough for him that had an impact on his company. He became a SPEED evangelist by spreading the word about the benefits of shifting to a fast and flexible talent strategy. The result? His company no longer took months to find talent, and many more projects were successful. Integrating SPEED within your organization may be seamless or challenging depending on your company's cultural perspectives and internal processes; you might encounter a few roadblocks and/or some minor speed bumps along the way.

Perhaps you think the SPEED strategy would work for other companies but doesn't apply to your business—actually, that's a mental roadblock right there. I see many people who encounter roadblocks often, whether it is mindset, organizational, structural, procedural, or political. For instance, roadblocks involving time, budget, and executive buy-in can occur at different stages of the journey, depending on the company.

Everyday I help managers and decision makers overcome various roadblocks in order to drive their business forward by building efficient on-demand teams. Let's review these roadblocks and learn how to get past them. I know that you can make an impact by overcoming the roadblocks.

Roadblocks

Consultants Are Too Expensive

"We just can't afford a consultant." Ah yes, let's address the elephant in the room. There is a pervasive perception that consultants are overpriced mercenaries who create pretty

PowerPoints but don't do much work. I have seen this misperception many times. Does that mean there isn't any truth to it? Unfortunately, as in any profession, there are some consultants who overpromise and under deliver, leaving you with the sinking feeling that you've been taken advantage of. I have worked with clients who complained about the money they had spent on consultants and the result was a "strategy" binder that merely collected dust on their bookshelf. Or they hired a large team of costly consultants from a reputable firm based on a senior executive's recommendation, but nothing much happened. Consultants are not created equal, and this is why I developed SPEED: to help you create the best team of on-demand consultants and get the most from them.

Consultant rates vary widely depending on their degree of expertise, particular discipline, industry, and/or capability. Also, their rates fluctuate depending on the supply and demand in local markets.

Another underlying perception related to consultant cost is that they are more expensive than equivalent FTEs. Managers see a consultant's bill rate and compare it to their company's salary structure. This isn't an accurate comparison, and it could lead to resentment towards the consultant. People have different ideas of what "expensive" is, so determining the rate is in many ways both an art and a science. It's important to assess the additional value the consultant brings to the project and the return on investment generated by the work.

As I noted in Chap. 4, when assessing salary rates, managers should include the fully-burdened cost of a FTE's salary as a point of comparison relative to the consultant's bill rate. The fully-burdened cost starts with the FTE's base salary, and then includes medical benefits, stock (if any), 401k contribution, office space, paid time off, employer taxes, state and federal taxes, and other costs the company incurs for that employee.

A powerful benefit of on-demand teams as well as managing deliverables by project is that you can manage your costs more efficiently by allocating resources to a variable cost line rather than as a fixed cost. For public companies, headcount is a large fixed cost and a driver of earnings per share (EPS). On the other hand, bringing in talent on a contract basis is a variable cost that does not impact the EPS, thus enabling you to dynamically manage your talent needs without a substantial impact to the company's fixed costs.

In addition, take into account the knowledge transfer, value-add aspects, and intangibles that the expert brings to the project's team. Those are difficult to quantify on a balance sheet, but can be invaluable to the company. The value of a consultant is much more than just a number. The intangibles and expertise that the team will gain may far exceed what you initially anticipate. I had a client once tell me his consultant made his team better. When I inquired more about what specifically she did, he said that her expertise in communications added a discipline and rigor that he was unaware he needed until she began working with him. None of us can be experts in everything, so trusting an expert to bring value may open your eyes to what is possible and raise the bar for everyone on your team.

A great consultant leaves the team better off than when the project began—whether it's by improving a process with solid project management skills, by establishing the key analytics that the team will rely upon to make important decisions, or by educating the team about online channels and techniques.

I Don't Have the Budget

"All my budget is allocated already." Sometimes budgets may be locked up in the form of retainers with an existing agency. You can always choose to reallocate funds to drive the most important business goals. Many companies work with large agencies on retainer; but I'm often surprised that managers and executives aren't measuring the return on investment (ROI) with respect to their agency retainers. This is something that should be reviewed on a continuing basis. Also, managers and executives might not have a solid understanding of the expertise level of individuals at the agency who are working on their account.

Ask these questions: are you really getting the most value? Is this agency helping you drive business? How do you know you are maximizing your results? In Chap. 4, I noted that some companies are moving away from agencies with multimillion dollar retainers; instead, they are bringing in individual experts who are more nimble, and at a fraction of the price they paid the agency. As noted previously, I worked with a large online company that saved thousands of dollars each month by replacing an outside agency with in-house consultants who worked on its project. Not only did the company save money, replacing the agency with in-house consultants added more value and got things done faster.

In reality, you most likely have the funds. Experiment with a small project by taking a fraction of the budget to bring in an expert. This way you'll test the waters and determine if you can drive better results with a consultant focused only on the project. One successful project using consultants usually begets another, with the added benefit of moving your business forward.

Internal Policies and Gatekeepers

"I can't get buy-in." Implementing a new approach isn't always easy, especially in large, seemingly slow-to-move companies. In a future chapter you will meet Roberta, a former senior executive, who was brought into a company to transform its B2B division. She immediately hit a roadblock as she started building her team: the specialized talent agency she wanted to work with wasn't currently on the company's approved vendor list. It took some persuasion and hoop jumping to get the consultants she wanted cleared, but once she did, the quality of the new talent quickly proved the usefulness of her idea: to work within the company's boundaries while delivering business value.

You might need a person more senior than you to convince company gatekeepers to add a name to the approved vendor list or to get past other internal policies. Resistance can be overcome with allies pushing for needed changes—even though others are against it or would rather keep things as they are. Make the business case for the move and couch it in terms of a short-term, limited investment "pilot" project that can easily end if the results aren't there. By starting small in this way, hesitant executives are taking on very little risk in comparison to the potential reward. Also, beginning with a "win" builds trust, and that sets the stage to do more projects with consultants.

We've Always Hired Employees

"Everything is working just fine. I have my team and we are hitting our goals. Why would I rock the boat and bring in outsiders?" The status quo is usually the path of least resistance and does not enable you to innovate and move forward. It's easy to have the attitude that "I don't want to bring in outsiders" or "I'll just stick with what I have."

I challenge you to review your goals and to ask yourself if you are doing everything you can to encourage agility and add value to your organization. Managers looking to make an impact can be viewed, for good or bad, as "change agents" within their companies, especially when pushing for the nimbleness that comes with bringing in project-based experts. What more could you do if you had access to a wider range of on-demand resources? You might launch a new product, expand into a new channel, grow overseas, or perhaps redefine your industry. Integrating on-demand experts into your team enables you to do more, go farther, grow, and expand.

Employers should not overlook the importance of a fresh perspective. For a critical project, especially one that's innovative or outside the mold of what's previously been done in your company, it can be a great asset to have someone who's been exposed to different insights and experiences that your FTEs might not have. The best leaders know they need people who not only understand the needs of a project, but are also able to spot additional needs and challenges they themselves haven't thought of. That's the benefit of bringing in an expert; they can help forecast, troubleshoot, and innovate in ways that you might not realize you need.

For example, I worked with a manager who believed that he could increase his company's channel partners' sales if he provided more training for them. He decided to bring in an expert as an experiment to test his theory that more training would drive more revenue. Not only did he benefit from the consultant's experience to get the project up and running quickly, he didn't have to burden or distract his team of FTEs, all of whom had heavy workloads. If his theory didn't pan out, he wouldn't have taken an employee off other critical projects or wasted that FTE's time. In addition, if the pilot project failed, it would not leave a mark on an FTE's job performance. This program eventually became one of the key revenue drivers and became a best practice within other areas of the company.

"It seems too risky to hire a consultant." If a company has not previously brought in on-demand consultant(s) for strategic projects, there likely will be resistance from an operational and cultural perspective. You will probably have to build a solid case for the consultant's role.

What works well in organizations where consultants are not commonly used is to connect a project's goals to clear deliverables that only an expert can provide. Also, a short-term contract, say for three months, is a great way to test the consultant option with little risk. Usually if you can make a business case to management about an important project and have the budget to execute it, they will give you a chance. Some considerations in making a business case include the opportunity costs of failing to bring in an expert: the time it will take to go to market or to hire in the traditional way. Sometimes articulating what likely won't happen is as important as predicting what could happen.

One of the great selling points of hiring an experienced consultant is that they are comfortable navigating in a cross-functional organization. They often are adept at extracting order out of chaotic situations and at winning people over. There is acceptance and trust once employees can see that the expert(s) are there to help and not take their jobs or make their lives more difficult.

Company leaders often recognize the value of consultants because they see that the consultants can serve as the bridge that joins different teams, groups, and business lines or locations together. I have observed instances in which two or more groups within a company did not work well together, so a consultant was brought in as a project manager and facilitator. A consultant/project manager is an excellent solution because he or she is not on anyone's side: their purpose is to deliver results on the project.

"I worry about cultural fit." Consultants can and do work well within different company cultures; it's part of their skillset. As noted in Chap. 4, you should understand the company's culture and who would work well with your team on the project. For example, is your company community driven? Does it have an entrepreneurial spirit? What types of personalities will mesh well with your team? This knowledge works for you, the team, and the consultant. If the consultant had previously worked successfully in entrepreneurial environments, for example, or in cultures similar to yours, the "cultural fit" question probably won't be an issue. During the interview process, you should have received examples concerning their background in similar roles, either as a FTE or as a contractor, and how they would accomplish the project goals while working within your company's culture.

"How do I integrate strong, experienced consultants with my FTE team so that everyone works together as an efficient unit?" Building strong blended teams of FTEs and consultants, with top to bottom buy-in, is a critical component of the integration process. In Chap. 4, I noted that full-time employees must see consultants not as "outsiders" or someone taking

over their jobs. Your FTEs should understand that the roles of the expert or team of experts will add value to everyone, and the future of the company. Strong communication and transparency will help the new integrated team get off to a smooth start, while avoiding friction or resentment from developing.

As mentioned in the case of Green Company (see Chap. 8), "We did have weekly calls," noted Diana, who managed a large transformation project for the company. "We also had weekly team meetings. At one point, probably for several months, we had daily rah-rahs at 7:30 a.m. every morning. We would have 30 people in a room and we'd say, okay, this is what we're doing. This is the focus. Here's the countdown to the next big point."[1]

Even in smaller organizations, with only one or two consultants on a project, it is equally important to build a spirit of team camaraderie or there can be conflict. "There was definitely conflict," Diana noted. "It was tough. I ended up losing some people to other departments because it was an environment that was very difficult and high pressure." Diana went on to that eventually most of the team realized that the knowledge transfer was necessary so that the consultants could be productive.

Your Plate Is Full

"I'm way too busy." I hear this almost every day from managers and executives. It seems like everything is in crisis mode.

Even worse, you're reacting to those crisis situations without taking time for reflection as things fly at you. You realize you need help, and fast. Sound all too familiar? Then, when you finally do reach out to your network or contact a talent agency and you get a list of suitable candidates to consider, you still don't act. Why? Because your hair's on fire, and too often you are forced to tackle problems only once they become urgent.

There is no way to end this cycle unless you pause and put some thought into defining what it will take to successfully complete the important projects that are crying out for immediate attention. Prioritization is a must when you are overwhelmed. When my brain feels so full that it's going to explode, I write every task down on a sheet of paper. Simply taking 15 minutes to get my tasks written down helps me to prioritize effectively.

When you're in a "solve it right now" mode, unrealistic expectations about deliverables can emerge. By carving out planning time, you can identify your priorities, and you might see that an expert can take some of the workload off your plate. One advantage of bringing in a consultant to help clear your plate is that onboarding is faster than hiring an FTE. Also, the consultant's sole focus is the successful completion of the project with the desired outcomes you've determined.

Managers often tell me that bringing on an expert to run an important program or project also relieves pressure, freeing him or her to think about the next project that has the potential to deliver even more value to the organization.

Consultants Aren't As Loyal As FTEs

"Consultants can't be 'all in' because they are not employees. Loyalty is bought with a consistent paycheck and by offering employees stock options." Or, *"How can I know they'll be loyal to my company?"* These are concerns I hear about consultants that simply are not true.

These are understandable concerns. But here is the truth: gaining "loyalty" in the business world isn't dependent on how someone gets paid. Many employers operate under the belief that their employees work a certain number of hours per week, under certain standard terms, for the promise of a regular paycheck, healthcare benefits, and an eventual pension or stock options/awards. But here's the problem: without those "loyalty" perks, can you ensure they'll act in your company's best interest? How can you know they won't simply be looking out for themselves? How can you really trust them? Those are complicated questions to be sure, but buying loyalty is never a good strategy.

Another common misperception among some employers is that consultants are no more than highly paid temps—that they're in and out, and how can they be loyal to your company when they will move on to other companies and projects soon enough?

Loyalty means having the best interests of the business at heart and caring about the quality and results of the work. Can loyalty really be "bought," whether through stock options or other perks? Employees might be "resting and vesting," waiting to cash out and move on the next opportunity. These employees may not be invested in the success of the company and so have questionable loyalty. If an employee is simply putting in the time necessary to exercise stock options, that's not loyalty. As Amanda, a technology company manager, noted, "I've heard people tell me, 'Well, I'm staying until February, that's when I get my stock options.' That's not loyalty—it's loyalty to the stock options."[2]

There are different ways to view loyalty. Consultants are loyal to the projects they work on because their reputations and businesses depend on producing great outcomes. They are not jockeying for the next promotion or involved in office politics. Consultants are there to get the job done without drama, stock option-loyalty, and HR headaches.

Consultants want to work on projects where their role makes a difference. Even in a short-term situation, they are loyal to the project's success and delivering on what they were hired to do—not a consistent paycheck or stock options.

"Often times, I actually end up with more loyalty with consultants I have worked with over the years than I do with a FTE. This is because consultants are able to come in and do a very specific thing, plus you often need the same expertise over and over again, depending on where you are," Amanda, an IT executive, said.

Amanda's comments strike me as another aspect of loyalty: It's not unusual for managers like Amanda, who change roles frequently within a company, to bring in their personal network of consultants as they move around.

Daniel, a young systems engineer, noted, "In general, I'm more loyal than many of my FTE peers because I have the opportunity to prove myself, and the autonomy to work the way I want to work."[3]

While misperceptions about consultant loyalty are starting to unravel, they remain a roadblock that companies must overcome if they want to build on-demand teams. If we're being honest with ourselves, we should recognize that loyalty is no longer defined the way it was in bygone eras when a person worked for one company until retirement. The Bureau of Labor Statistics[4] has estimated the average worker spends no more than four to five years with a single company.

Consultants know their personal brand and current reputation is everything, and doing great work may lead to future projects or referrals. They're invested in your success because it directly correlates to their success, and that only increases their drive and "loyalty" to do everything they can for your company.

Loyalty is not earned with a regular paycheck or stock options. Loyalty is earned through relationships based on trust and mutual success.

Consultants Can't Be Privy to Confidentiality

"How can I trust that these consultants aren't going to take our ideas to our competition?" This is a big issue in highly competitive industries where the same top consultants are constantly recruited. The best way to protect intellectual property is to perform a thorough due diligence review of the talent companies you choose to partner with and of your consultants. Make sure your legal team has solid non-disclosure agreements (NDAs) and/or confidentiality agreements. In order to know who you are working with, you may want to do a background check as well.

When hiring a consultant, be sure to put in place a master service agreement that includes terms that describe how everyone will work together and that has a section regarding confidentiality.

Samantha, a project manager/consultant, says that she tries to clear confidentiality issues up as soon as she meets with somebody that she will work with. She lets them know that they "can talk about and collaborate on the project with the same sense of confidentiality and security that you expect from an employee." She informs them of her own confidentiality agreement with the company and that she has a long-standing history of being trusted.

I'm Not Comfortable with a Consultant Working Remotely

"How do I really know what they are doing if I can't see them?" Some managers need to see the people who work for them every day in order to know they are committed and doing the work.

These managers make sure their employees arrive on time and are at their desk until 5 p.m. But this management style is not geared to attracting the best and brightest—the people who want autonomy, purpose, and mastery—according to Dan Pink in his book *Drive*.[5]

Take for example, Daniel from Chap. 2, a consultant for a software company.[6] He emphasizes the importance of autonomy and independence within his peer group. Rather than the "very hands on, breathes-down-your-neck" type of management style that he feels is all too present in traditional positions, his experience is one where he is able to work at his own pace and without constant supervision. Instead of wasting time answering to several managers about the same project at the cost of actually working, he is trusted to meet deadlines and get the job done.

Daniel, a Millennial, believes that he is not alone among his peers, who want the same level of independence that they had in college. Consulting allows autonomy and the ability to "do very well with limited direction and the opportunity to exercise that creative muscle."

Speaking about the win-win advantages of consulting, Daniel suggested that "rewarding people with autonomy is a key thing for managers to consider, and part of that includes the ability for remote work. I think that's a huge perk. I find that I can spend some extra time on deliverables when needed, if I'm not dealing with the commute."

Removing the perception that team members must be constantly monitored frees everyone to be more efficient and to do their best work. Consultants can drive business results faster without being micromanaged. Everyone can work this way if corporate culture shifts to recognizing the value of the contributions and results over constant face time and physical presence. It is important to develop relationships, but once you have done that, don't micromanage.

Agility, rapid response, expert help when needed for as long as needed—the on-demand workforce provides all of that. SPEED unlocks the potential that the new opportunities of the workplace present.

The previous chapter described SPEED; and this chapter has outlined some of the roadblocks to adopting SPEED to build on-demand teams as well as the shift in perspective than can enable you to see past those roadblocks. The next chapters showcase some real-world examples of companies that have creatively deployed on-demand teams to drive innovation, reduce cost, and get results.

Notes

1. Quotes are from interviews conducted in September 2014. Person and company names changed.
2. Personal interview, August 25, 2015. Name is changed.
3. Quotes are from personal interviews, October 2015. Names changed.
4. "Employee Tenure in 2014," U.S. Bureau of Labor Statistics. Press release, September 18, 2014. Retrieved November 11, 2015, at http://www.bls.gov/news.release/pdf/tenure.pdf

5. Dan Pink, *Drive: The Surprising Truth About What Motivates Us* (New York: Riverhead Books, 2011). Also see Chap. 2 for further discussion.
6. Personal interview, October 2015.

CHAPTER 6

A Start-Up Within a Corporation

*T*his was one of my first problems to solve—how am I going to bring these really strong high performers together in a way that we can call ourselves a team, even though they might not even intersect with each other? How do I want to mix and augment staffing strategy?

—*Roberta M., senior manager*

The real-world stories in the following chapters take you behind the scenes of companies that have leveraged the power of on-demand experts to solve their specific challenges. They all hit some roadblocks, whether it was internal buy-in or integration issues, but they prevailed and were successful. Let's look at what Blue Company accomplished.

Blue Company's[1] chief executive officer was on the brink of something big. He saw exciting changes ahead for his wireless carrier, but he needed help to navigate the twists and turns in the road to disruptively "zig" while his competitors were "zagging."

He wanted to ignite a new "movement" within Blue, to shake up his company as well as the entire industry. He didn't see his company as just another status quo player in the wireless market. He wanted to position Blue as an outside-the-box disruptor in both the consumer division and its business-to-business (B2B) division.

The movement required recreating Blue's products by driving greater transparency and giving customers more options to customize pricing plans. They successfully did this for the consumer division, but it was time for the B2B department to adopt the new plans as well as tailor them to their B2B customers. The new plans would align the "movement" as envisioned by the CEO.

This was a perfect opportunity for someone with a new perspective and proven entrepreneurial skills to step in and work with Blue's existing teams to adapt the consumer initiatives to align with the B2B customers.

The CEO reached out to Roberta, a former Blue manager. The CEO's call came at just the right time for her. "When the CEO called me, I had run my own successful marketing company for more than six years," the dynamic entrepreneur related. "However, I was getting pretty exhausted running my own company, especially in the ever-changing marketing space, and I was ready for a return to corporate America."

The situation, and resulting fit, had an air of inevitability: Roberta was ready for a change but also wanted to continue working in an entrepreneurial, start-up-type environment. Things advanced quickly. "I was hired in less than a week to return to Blue and develop and then implement as many as 56 different initiatives over 18 months that would remake the B2B division's marketing, pricing plans and relationships with customers. It was a compelling and interesting project; it was, in effect, a start-up inside a large corporation."

"When I got hired, I was left to myself to figure out what I was going to do. How do I want to mix and augment my staffing strategy?" Roberta noted. "I looked around thinking, 'Who do I want to work with?' Because I had just come from managing my own company, I thought differently than the typical employee who maybe had never run their own business. I knew I would create the team I wanted and not simply try to make this happen with the team I had. So, I moved some full-time employees to different roles they were better suited for and brought on the experts I needed to get the job done."

"What we were going to do is change the industry," she explained. "I needed A-players with backgrounds in wireless that could get up to speed very quickly." The tasks weren't easy; "We were constantly 'on' and had to deliver, and deliver with excellence," Roberta said. "I needed these A-players yesterday."

Roberta opted to use a specialized talent agency she trusted to provide her with the on-demand experts that were needed. The agency she chose to work with wasn't on the company's approved vendor list, however. This was one of the first roadblocks she encountered. It took some persuasion and hoop-jumping to get the talent agency cleared, but once she did, the quality of the talent this agency gave her quickly proved how worthwhile her new strategy was.

While working with the talent agency, Roberta focused on the potential consultants' soft skills, proven successes on other projects, emotional intelligence, and competency in their field.

The consultant onboarding process featured kick-off meetings, communication protocols, schedules and clarity around cultural fit, soft skills, work scope, and roles. The onboarding went smoothly, but then she hit another roadblock. "Initially, no one was collaborating very well with each other," Roberta noted.

She asked herself how she could create a strong team camaraderie among the experts she had brought in and Blue's full-time employees. It was a fast-paced and high-pressure environment that Roberta compared to a college dormitory where everyone is cramming for a college exam at the last minute. She gathered the team together and had them whiteboard the vision and strategy for the B2B transformation. "This wasn't easy, but the full-time employees' schedules were maxed-out, so they understood we needed the consultants and that it was in their best interest to work as a team or we would not be successful. Eventually, we all felt we were in a start-up environment. I worked hard to foster a close knit team—everyone felt they were in this together."

Roberta finally had a team of A-listers, both consultants and the FTEs, who worked as a lean, nimble, and strongly connected group—a true "start-up" within Blue. "We are also very diverse. We have age diversity. We've got culture diversity, race diversity, sexual preference diversity. I liked working with such a diverse team and the diverse perspective they brought to the table. Diversity adds value in terms of new ideas and fresh perspectives, which encourages innovative thinking and more ways to connect with a wide range of groups of all ages, interests and backgrounds."

Blue's B2B project was unlike any other large initiative the company had undertaken before, and it posed some unique challenges. Fortunately, Roberta's willingness to adapt and innovate "on her feet" rather than playing by the corporate rulebook allowed her to meet these challenges head-on and address them before they became larger issues.

As a result, Blue's once-stalled B2B focus was transformed at the moderate cost of about $2.5 million for six consultants over the course of 18 months. The B2B division re-engaged with their customers, gained new relevance in the marketplace, and had fully embraced the CEO's mission of "shaking things up"—not only in their industry, but within the company itself. The innovative start-up within Blue's company, aided by the efforts of Roberta and her team of consultants and FTEs, was a significant contribution to Blue's rapid growth as a market leader.

Note

1. Story is based on actual events; interviews were conducted in September and November 2014 and December 2015. Company, locations, person names, and some minor details are changed.

CHAPTER 7

An Innovative Idea That Launched a $100 Million Business

I decided to take a small risk and test my idea of building a training program that would help educate our channel partners and our own people.

—*Roger T, VP, Red Inc.*

Roger, an innovator and problem solver, had an unusual idea. He didn't have executive buy-in and not much budget for it, but he decided to go ahead and test the idea anyway, rather stealthily. His hunch would eventually pay off and transform an entire division, becoming a company-wide program for thousands of Red's sales partners.

As a senior VP at Red Inc.,[1] a large multinational technology company, Roger believed he was facing one of his toughest challenges: sales and support for computers and software was changing dramatically, and as a result, Red's channel partners' business model was not keeping pace with the times. This was a problem that Red and many other technology companies faced at this time. Red's channel partners were focused mainly on selling computer repair and software help, but technology products were evolving to the point where customers no longer had as many problems that required repair and/or software help. Customers could handle most issues themselves because equipment and software were more reliable and much easier to use. The channel partners were telling Roger and the rest of the company, "We used to know how to sell your stuff, but we don't know how to do it effectively anymore." Red wanted to help its sales channel partners; doing so meant that they would have to reinvent their business model.

"This was in the early 2000s when the move away from making money simply on hardware was really underway," Roger said. Like many large successful companies, Red did things the so-called "Red Way"—in other words, the way they were always done. Roger also noted that large companies "can sometimes get kind of closed off to what is happening in the world and what might apply to them." For example, he said that during this time Red didn't have extensive experience with software as a service (SaaS) and related cloud-based services. As a result, some of their products and services weren't adapting fast enough to market and technological changes.

"The way for the partners to make money in this evolving market now was not by just selling products but also by delivering added value by increasing sales through support services, closer engagement and going beyond the initial transaction," Roger explained. "I decided to take a small risk by testing my idea of building a training program that would help educate our channel partners to this, as well as our own people.

"But I was traveling 80 percent of the time and managing 400 people internationally; I had recently hired a new business manager, Sheila, so I put her in charge of implementing my idea, which I called Project X. It didn't take me long to realize she was having a hard time putting it together," Roger said.

The team at Roger's disposal wasn't properly equipped to bring the project to life or at the speed the project required. "They were busy with many other projects and I didn't want them distracted. This was new territory and something Red had never done before, so my team had no experience with this. They were also used to doing things according to Red Way's usual operational methods and procedures—Project X was side project that did not fit that mold."

Roger realized he needed outside talent—someone that could bring new ways of thinking and expertise on how to make Project X work. The project needed people who had experience with SaaS, social media, and how to educate the channel partners on selling online self-services. He also needed someone who would carry out his vision for the project without daily supervision, someone to whom he could say, "Here is what I want to achieve. Go make it happen," and trust that it would be done correctly. He needed a person who could read between the lines and make suggestions that he had not thought about.

Roger had some budget available, about $100,000, for the project. He turned to Laurie, who owned a specialized talent agency. He knew Laurie from a previous project and was confident that she and her on-demand cadre of experts could handle the various aspects of Project X as it progressed. Laurie did the initial work to move the idea forward and mapped out a plan on how to develop and communicate the training program with the channel partners. Then Laurie hit a roadblock.

Her effectiveness was unintentionally limited because Roger had Laurie reporting to the same business manager who was unable to succeed with Roger's vision initially: Sheila. And Sheila had her own agenda. She was stuck in a common corporate mindset: how she was perceived within Red. Her own acumen and individual success were more important to her than the success of Project X. Sheila's resentment, insecurity, and/or her need to prove her worth to the company all combined to hinder Laurie's effectiveness. Sheila did not communicate well or often enough with Laurie, failed to share critical information with her, and did not report on Project X updates to Roger. As a result, Laurie was handicapped and Project X was stalled for many months.

Once he discovered what was going on, Roger moved quickly to fix the issue by transferring Sheila to another department. He then empowered Laurie and her team of consultants to operate independently, reporting directly to him. That's when things started moving.

"This project reminded me of the importance of mindset when it comes to putting together an effective team. There's no room for ego, competition or power struggles; everyone must operate as a team and work towards the same goal rather than worrying over boosting their own professional reputation," Roger reflected.

Resentment is a common roadblock to success, as it was for Project X. Your team needs people who are willing to adapt and be flexible, with everyone doing their jobs to the best of their ability. They need to embrace the fact that when consultants are brought in, they are often there because they have skills that the existing team might not have and their expertise benefits the team and the entire company.

"Laurie's team not only finished the project for us, they transferred the knowledge the company would need to manage and expand the program company wide." It turned out to be an asset that the entire company could—and would—use.

Red's Project X-related business, which had been declining, grew by about $25 million in two years—and that was just in one region.

Roger's idea, a low-risk, $100,000 test for the company, was launched by on-demand talent and eventually migrated to other parts of the world and grew into a $100 million business.

Note

1. Story is based on actual events; interviews were conducted in September 2014. Company, locations, person names, and some minor details are changed.

CHAPTER 8

Orchestrating a Global Transformation with On-Demand Experts

*T*he contractors were here to help solve a problem. You need to come to me and let me know if we're not doing things right. You're here because you have that expertise. You have done this before. We haven't. You have to really empower those people to let them help you solve the problem.

—*Diana S., Green Company*

Green Company, a well-established and highly respected insurance company with a long history in its industry, decided to replace a legacy system with a new, customized computer administration system. This set in motion a company-wide transformation project for Green, which was named Project A.[1] Project A would eventually impact every department and functionality in the global organization and more than 1000 people at a projected cost of $75–$100 million over two to three years.

The company's entire back-office operation was an antiquated system that stretched back to the 1980s. The system was delaying the company's time to market for new products, negatively impacting policy changes, pricing changes, and much more. It was so old there was very little technical support or replacement hardware available. Another complicating and challenging factor was that Green's IT platform was a system originally built in Europe that its corporate headquarters was trying to shoehorn into use across all of its business divisions, including Europe, South America, the U.S., and Asia. Simply put: it was long past its prime and didn't work effectively anymore.

Diana, whose take-charge demeanour that was inspiring and friendly, was recruited out of Green's East Coast office. She was placed in charge of a new Midwest division as vice president of business change, and her main assignment was to facilitate the Project A transformation.

Diana began building a team, placing people that were doing similar jobs in different departments on the project. She had to pull people from each company division in order to use their specific knowledge, most of these team members ended up doing their regular day jobs while working on Project A.

"When we started Project A," Diana said, "we were using only internal staff and everybody was doing double duty, so they were doing their own jobs and then they were also working on this project. We also went through a long process of getting the internal staffing approved."

But Diana eventually saw that Green did not have enough people with the proper expertise in place to make the transformation happen. In addition to stretching the company's current team to the breaking point, many did not have the project management experience and skillsets that Project A required. "When the project was first under consideration, the IT Department knew immediately it would need extra headcount to support the project," she said. "But it also became clear within a few months that IT needed expert outside help."

Fortunately, it was not a hard sell to get executive-level buy-in to bring in outside help for Project A. "Green's CEO was involved and supportive of the people and the process," Diana said. "Once the validation process was finalized, we received the authorization to slowly start adding outside help. It became clear to the team that the consultants would give us the flexibility to scale up or down quickly. Unlike with full-time employees, we were able to quickly remove individuals that were not needed or weren't a good fit for the project."

"This was a company that did things one way for a long time, so there were obstacles to bringing on consultants and integrating them into the company culture and team." Diana continued. "For one thing, Green employees tend to have long careers with Green, and those onboard for 20-plus years had trouble thinking differently, beyond the way things had always been done, so there were some big obstacles." Diana recalled that senior executives were always talking about the bench. "How do you build your bench?" A project of this scope required seasoned project managers and specific technology skills along with process and policy management skills. It became clear that Diana's "bench" was very thin. This was her first obstacle.

She also realized that she would need an experienced leader to drive and facilitate the day-to-day operation of the project. That meant looking beyond current Green employees. "Not to denigrate them because they were certainly skilled in their roles, but this transformational project definitely needed an outsider with a different perspective," she said.

Another obstacle was the inflexibility of the company's culture. Diana described Green as a company where "people had been in roles that don't change much, and consequently they had difficulty with change. For instance, a small thing that turned into a significant issue was the fact that if an employee worked at home on certain days, they couldn't embrace the revised schedule needed for Project A. I told them you're going to have to be more flexible. You might not be able to work at home every Friday."

Initially there was resistance about bringing on consultants to implement the new system. Green had to overcome those concerns and fears. "We really had to tell the whole story about what the system would look like when it was done and how bringing in the outside expertise would make everyone's job easier and better for the organization. We (Green) could get products to market faster, we would sell more products, and as a result, there would be more jobs." Diana and other senior managers emphasized to the staff that bringing on consultants for Project A was good for them, the company, and the futures of both.

"But there was definitely conflict," she noted. "It was tough. I ended up losing some people to other departments because the environment was very high pressure. Ultimately, most of the team realized that we needed the help so desperately they became focused on sitting down and transferring as much knowledge and information as possible so that the consultants could be super productive."

Another obstacle was getting senior management to speak with a consistent voice when they communicated with their managers and department staff; everyone had to be committed to the project. They had to come together and say, "Okay, here's the amount of work that we think it's going to be in IT. Here's the amount of work we think is going to be in Operations. Here's how much money we need. Here's how many people we need. Here are the positive changes that we think we're going to have."

When it came to bringing in outside talent, Diana knew what she needed: individuals who could align with Green's culture, who were also able to hit the ground running and who had the diplomatic skills to work well with long-time employees. That said, it wasn't an easy road because they needed the talent and fast. Diana explained, "I needed a broad range of on-demand experts in several different industries, so I turned to several industry-specific talent agencies; they were agile, highly responsive and quickly helped me find the most skilled and qualified people in IT, process mapping and project management, etc." At this stage of the project, onboarding the consultants with those skills turned into a team effort. The onboarding began by including various company divisions in the interview process. "These individuals detailed the various project roles, expectations and Green's cultural idiosyncrasies," Diana said.

On-boarding was a highly collaborative process that each department manager participated in. They all agreed what the on-boarding would look like: how the consultants would be integrated and managed. How? The same as FTEs: the consultants weren't seen as outsiders by the department heads and the employees followed suit. By doing so, they integrated a diverse group with the specialized skills needed to implement Project A successfully. The CEO, members of the senior management team, and the project management office (PMO) specifically detailed Project A's scope, the challenges involved, and the desired outcome. "I also wanted to make sure the consultants understood how their experience would benefit the organization, and how their specific skills, competencies and capabilities would add value. And I wanted them to understand that they could provide honest, constructive feedback and solutions."

Some consultants were hired to take over key day-to-day roles within several departments in order to free up the staff members whose expertise was needed for Project A. This helped build camaraderie as the full-time employees were in charge of training the consultants to take over the normal responsibilities and getting them up to speed.

Because veteran employees were included in the interviewing process and in the final selection of the consultants, Green's employees came to see the consultants not as "outsiders" or people "taking over" their jobs. Green employee commitment and involvement was vital because "they knew the system, they knew the products, they knew the culture, they knew the business," Diana said.

Overall, approximately 30–50 consultants were brought in during the course of the project. Diana estimated the consultants worked on the project at various times for one year. Of the 57 people working on Project A, 28 were consultants at a cost of $2.1 million. Each department had at least one or two outside experts brought in to support the project or to backfill the existing FTE count. The PMO had seven consultants working on the project, IT had nine consultants and Operations between five and ten. Several of the IT experts had the technical background and project management experience to help Green's IT department document current and end-result processes, including developing requirements. Two of the PMO consultants were experts in process mapping, which helped to identify and document requirements and processes, and facilitate focus groups. Other consultants were certified project managers with experience managing complex projects, including resource allocation, scheduling, and budgeting plans.

The project began to build momentum. "We did have weekly calls," Diana said. "We also had weekly team meetings. For several months, we had daily rah-rahs at 7 a.m. every morning. We would have 30 people in a room and say, okay, this is what we're doing. This is the focus. Here's the countdown to the next big point."

Under Green's flexible talent strategy, Diana was empowered to address problems as they arose before they could seriously affect the project. A case in point regarding flexibility: the consultant Diana initially chose to run the day-to-day operation of Project A was not the right fit—something she realized shortly after he started work on the project. "Within four to six weeks, I saw that he wasn't getting the job done; it wasn't working out, so I just let him go."

In contrast, it's much more difficult to let FTEs go, Diana noted. "It's a long process to have to go through and weed them out, especially in an organization like Green. It takes time. At other companies I've had people on performance plans for a year before I was able to let them go." For Diana, the ability to move fast to resolve the situation for Project A was perfect.

Because this person was a consultant, she was able to move quickly to bring on the right person, adopting a "fail fast and win" mentality. "Firing a full-time employee would have been more costly in terms of money and time," Diana said. "And then, the cost of having the wrong person heading up the project during the extensive time it would take to remove an FTE would have done irreparable harm."

The results? At its completion, Project A allowed the company to bring products to market faster, and at the right price points to be more competitive. In addition, the knowledge transfer to Green's employees lasted long past the consultant's time with Green. This also prevented training, support, and workflow issues from arising after the consultants left. Diana and other senior managers were able to successfully orchestrate a transformation of this magnitude by accessing and leveraging the on-demand expertise Green needed.

Note

1. Story is based on actual events; interviews were conducted in September 2014 and December 2015. Company, locations, person names, and some minor details are changed.

CHAPTER 9

Conclusion

*I*t is not the strongest species that survive, nor the most intelligent, but the ones most responsive to change.

Charles Darwin

Change is the only thing that is certain, and there's no end to the changes occurring in the workplace and workforce. This book has shown you that the on-demand workplace is here to stay, and it will continue to gain momentum.

All companies want teams made up of the best and brightest talent. To achieve that, companies must embrace the reality that the best and brightest most likely won't want to be on your team unless you update your talent strategy. Why? By 2020 there will be 65 million freelancers and consultants choosing how, when, and where they want to work. Innovative managers, executives, and companies will have to find new ways to access and bring on these millions of freelancers and consultants.

If you brought together a group of CEOs, industry leaders, and visionaries to brainstorm about how to achieve success, it would be unanimous that without great talent there can be no success.

I've dispelled the common belief that there is a talent gap. However, if companies are unable to integrate this fast-growing workforce made up of freelancers and consultants seeking non-FTE roles with their existing teams, then they will experience a talent gap of their own making.

Remember the case of Borders in Chap. 1? The 40-year-old bookseller disappeared almost overnight in 2011 because it was too slow to recognize a changing book market that was moving rapidly to online sales and away from brick-and-mortar stores.

The lesson from the Borders story is that if you see a market disruption coming, you must be ready to make the leap to the new way of doing things quickly and decisively. Move to embrace the "obvious future," as it is called. Disrupt yourself before someone else does it for you.

By doing so, you might ask yourself, "What if I fail?" Often, we are in a state of trial and error as we deal with the roadblocks in work and in life. That's OK, because while the goal might be clear, the road to achieving it often is uncertain; the plan may have to change or be scrapped entirely.

I call this the cycle of "fail fast and win." When we are open to learning from our failures and challenges, we will see solutions to problems that we may not have seen before. Failure has a negative connotation, but in reality, failure is a necessary step toward eventual success.

In school, we were indoctrinated to avoid failure at all costs: failing a test, failing a class, failing to conform. The message was hardwired in us by the time we put on the cap and gown and accepted our diploma: failure was bad instead of what it actually is—a learning experience. Not embracing failure, or always avoiding risk by playing it safe, could be the costliest thing you can do.

If your company is like Borders and other companies that avoided failure by playing it safe and blindly adhering to the status quo like duct tape, you could, like them, get blown away by upstart companies and their more risk-tolerant competition.

Strategies constantly evolve. Projects change, and sometimes projects take on a life of their own or need modification based on business needs. For example, Blue Company's CEO had a vision that ultimately meant he needed to bring in someone—Roberta—with proven entrepreneurial skills to quickly align the B2B division's product offerings and customer pricing programs. Roberta's fresh perspective helped create a unique environment within Blue—a start-up in a sense, which implemented the B2B division's transformation.

The key is to remain flexible so that you can adapt as changes occur. This is part of SPEED's evaluation process.

Flexibility is a major part of the story in two other chapters of this book. What if Diana wasn't able to quickly replace the consultant she originally brought in to run Green Company's technology transformation project, but who turned out to be the wrong fit? Within four to six weeks, "I knew it wasn't a fit. He wasn't working out, and I just let him go," she said. Diana's flexibility to move fast to resolve the situation was perfect; because this person was a consultant, she was able to move quickly to bring on the right individual by adopting a "fail fast and win" mentality. A full-time employee would have been more expensive and harder to let go; this nimbleness was critical to the project's success.

And Roger, of Red Inc., faced a similar situation. He quickly pivoted to get the right talent in place after he had first assigned the wrong person—in this case, an FTE—to manage his innovative idea for a sales channel training program. He was able to change course quickly once the problem became evident. Eventually, his idea became a company-wide $100 million business.

Within the Green and Red stories, there was an initial failure—putting the wrong people in place—that could have led to an even larger failure if Diana and Roger had not had the insight to pivot quickly to correct their situations. They embraced a "failure" in the talent they had placed and did a course correction.

Using fail fast and win thinking, you could bring in a consultant for a short period of time, say 30 days, for a "test run" to determine whether that person is the right fit. If not, the problem can be resolved quickly before stalling or even derailing a project.

There's another benefit that comes with bringing in a consultant for a short period of time: a new perspective. The expert might see the flaws in a project and could recommend a solution before failure occurs, suggest an entirely new direction, or even to scratch the project all together.

Creating on-demand teams and adopting the SPEED strategy takes the ability to fail fast and win to a new level. Think of yourself as the conductor of an orchestra. You get to choose the musicians and the music for each concert. Some of the players might come and go, but you are always efficiently conducting your orchestra (team) to build an impactful and successful business.

That's navigating the talent shift.

Are you ready?

Resource Guide

The Resource Guide provides you with additional resources and information about the talent shift along with places where you can find experts to work on projects. It also lists some tips on how to evaluate a talent agency.

For more information and resources that will be updated frequently, go to: www.lisahufford.com/resources

Tips to Evaluate a Talent Agency

Proven Expertise Look at the agency's body of work and the results it has delivered to other companies. Get references from current or past clients in order to determine what their clients valued most about working with the agency. Determine what you are looking for in an agency? For example: if results and high value return are your key drivers (vs. big ideas), communicate this up front with the agency.

Talent Ask about how the agency finds and develops their talent. If you searching for expert talent and/or professionals in a particular industry, ask the agency to provide evidence that clearly demonstrates they have the particular talent in their database and that they are available.

Are they a "body shop" or are they focused on developing consultants? The best consultants are with agencies that showcase and value their expertise and invest in their growth. Find out how they motivate their talent. This is important because incentives can be for performing quality client work or accomplishing business development for the agency.

Business Model Ask about how the agency's projects are structured: are they deliverable or hourly? How do they measure success? What is their reporting cadence and does this coincide with your requirements for internal executives and/or stakeholders. How focused are they on analytics and how important are analytics to your business? You will want to see some reporting on a regular basis, so you will want an agency that can deliver reporting data. Finding an agency with standardized KPIs and SLAs is an important differentiator as well. If they don't have these metrics in place, find out how they measure success.

From Skillcrush on November 19, 2015

25 Top Sites for Finding the Freelance Jobs You Want

Cameron Chapman
(http://skillcrush.com/2015/11/19/25-top-sites-for-finding-freelance-jobs/)

Tech-Specific Job Boards

1. *Smashing Jobs*, part of Smashing Magazine, has a large listing of freelance tech jobs (they also have listings for full-time jobs). Smashing Jobs posts primarily developer jobs, though there are tons of designer jobs

listed, too. (http://jobs.smashingmagazine.com/ freelance)

2. The *Mashable Job Board* is devoted to digital and tech jobs around the world. They're used by some of the top companies in the world to find talent, including MTV News, Omaze, and more. Search for freelance in the keywords to find the appropriate listings. (http:// findjobs.mashable.com/)

3. *Coroflot* is specifically for creative jobs, with job postings from companies all over the world. They have a separate category for freelance work. In addition to web designer and developer jobs, they also list other creative and tech jobs. (http://www.coroflot.com/ jobs#job_levels=6)

4. *Working Nomads* is a curated list of remote jobs from companies around the world. Their job categories include design, development, sysadmin, customer success, management, and marketing. (http://www. workingnomads.co/)

5. *Authentic Jobs* lets you filter for freelance, contract, or moonlighting jobs from companies around the world. They have listings for everything from project managers to backend developers to content strategists. (https://authenticjobs.com/#types=7,3,2,6)

6. *GetACoder* is a great source for freelance developer jobs, as well as design and other tech-related work. They have tens of thousands of active jobs on the site, which can make narrowing down what to actually apply for a bit tricky. (http://www.getacoder. com/)

7. *WP Hired* is a great source if you're a WordPress pro looking for freelance work. They have a category just for freelance, and most of the jobs listed can be done from anywhere. There are a huge range of jobs on the site, from small plugin projects to complete redesigns. (http://www.wphired.com/#s=1%20target=)

8. *Problogger Jobs* is a job board just for bloggers that includes mostly freelance positions. A lot of the jobs are tech related, and WordPress and other tech skills are a huge advantage for anyone looking to blog. (http://jobs.problogger.net/)

9. *Krop* is a job board just for creatives. Krop sets itself apart from many others by letting you host your portfolio on their site, and is used by a number of high-profile creatives, such as photographer *Terry Richardson*, design agency *Heydeys*, and creative director *Eric Hoffman*. (http://www.krop.com/)

10. *Stack Overflow Careers* lists both full-time and contract positions. They mostly list developer and engineer jobs, though related fields are sometimes listed, too. (http://careers.stackoverflow.com/jobs?jobType=contract)

Members-Only Job Boards

11. *Traction* is a curated job board for marketers. Unlike many others, you have to apply and be accepted to be able to see jobs and projects posted on the site. (http://gotraction.com/)

12. *Matchist* is a curated job board for developers. They only accept 15% of the developers who apply, which makes them very appealing to those looking to hire.

If you're accepted, it can be a great way to find rewarding projects. (https://matchist.com/)

13. *Gigster* is a way for companies to hire development teams. They combine Silicon Valley-based product managers with elite developers from a vetted talent pool to take on customer projects. (https://www.try-gigster.com/)

14. *Folyo* is a members-only private community for finding freelance design jobs. Companies post their projects and then get a curated shortlist of designers who would be perfect for the job. (http://www.folyo.me/)

15. *OnSite* offers up curated freelancers for on-site and off-site jobs. Companies post a job, then get a list of freelancers who are a good match. Freelancers can post a bio and portfolio to appeal to those hiring. (http://onsite.io/)

16. *Gun.io* is a service that finds the best freelance developers for client projects. As a developer, you can apply with GitHub, so make sure you've got some great active projects there! (https://gun.io/)

17. *Crew* matches up companies with top designers and developers. Applying as a freelancer is as simple as submitting your name and online portfolio URL. (https://crew.co/)

18. *Hirable* is a self-curated community of developers used by companies like Google and Birchbox. Just sign up as a developer, set up your profile, and then set your availability (hirable, hirable soon, or busy). (https://wearehirable.com/)

19. *Envato Studio* hand-picks designers and developers for customer projects. For the most part, Envato actively looks for freelancers to add to Studio, but you can also submit a form to register your interest. (http://studio.envato.com/)

20. *Juiiicy* is a private community for top designers to find freelance projects. Rather than companies posting ads directly, other designers post inquiries they've gotten but can't or don't want to take on, and earn referral fees when another Juiiicy designer takes the job. (https://juiiicy.com/)

Other Job Boards

21. *LocalSolo* is a localized freelance job board for finding projects in your area. It's free to use as a freelancer and doesn't charge any commission, and you can customize your profile and work directly with clients from the start. (https://localsolo.com/)

22. *SimplyHired* lets you search for contract jobs in any location. They have thousands of job listings, though they're not limited to just tech jobs. Just search for the job title and optionally the city and state, and then refine the results to just include contract positions. (http://www.simplyhired.com/)

23. *Freelancer* is a huge job board specifically for freelance jobs. Much of the jobs listed on the site are tech jobs, with listings for designers, developers, marketers, SEO specialists, and more. (https://www.freelancer.com/)

24. *Upwork* is a large freelance job board that covers a huge variety of positions. There are job listings for web developers, designers, mobile developers, sales and marketing pros, and more. (https://www.upwork.com/)

25. *Guru* is another large freelance job board that includes tech as well as other positions. There are more jobs listed for tech and web than any other category, making it a good options for designers and developers. (http://www.guru.com/)

Bibliography

Collins, Jim. 2001. *Good to great: Why some companies make the leap...and others don't.* New York: HarperCollins Publishers Inc.

McKeown, Greg. 2014. *Essentialism: The disciplined pursuit of less.* New York: Crown Publishing Group.

Pink, Dan. 2011. *Drive: The surprising truth about what motivates us.* New York: Riverhead Books.

Index